Left at Fork.
4 Street on Right.
— Liberty Street
½ 920 Blue. Red Dodge
Shadow.

Training the Young Horse
The First Two Years

Training the Young Horse

The First Two Years

Anthony Crossley

Stanley Paul

London Sydney Auckland Johannesburg

Stanley Paul & Co. Ltd

An imprint of Century Hutchinson Ltd

Brookmount House, 62-65 Chandos Place,
Covent Garden, London WC2N 4NW

Century Hutchinson (Australia) Pty Ltd
89-91 Albion Street, Surry Hills,
New South Wales 2010, Australia

Century Hutchinson New Zealand Limited
191 Archers Road, PO Box 40-086, Glenfield, Auckland 10,
New Zealand

Century Hutchinson South Africa (Pty) Limited
PO Box 337, Bergvlei 2012, South Africa

First published 1978
Reprinted 1980, 1983, 1984, 1986, 1987, 1988, 1989

Set in Monotype Bembo

Printed and bound in Great Britain by
Anchor Press Ltd, Tiptree, Essex

ISBN 0 09 132420 3

Contents

Preface

This book is written in the hope that it will act as a useful guide to the less experienced rider who either has never before trained a young horse in basic dressage or has not trained a sufficient number of horses to be confident that he or she is treading the right path.

The ideas, theories and recommendations that follow are compounded from the author's personal experience of riding and more particularly from the verbal and written teaching of successful and sometimes famous exponents of the art of riding.

Nothing of importance in the book is an original invention or discovery by the author. Every expressed opinion or proposition of significance is supported by theories and practices that have been accepted as valid by those with the greatest experience in that sphere.

The author has attempted to co-ordinate this received knowledge in a form that can be easily assimilated, understood and put into practice by riders who have not yet had similar opportunities for practical study. It is intended to help them to progress smoothly and logically on sound lines and without unnecessary waste of time through all the essential stages of the basic education of a young horse on the flat. If the job is completed, the horse will be a comfortable, enjoyable and companionable ride and ready to face a more extended training in some specialized sphere.

The training advocated can and should be applied to all horses destined for any form of pleasure riding, that is to say for hunting,

The end result; a pleasure to ride. Colonel Alois Podhajsky on the author's horse, Valentine, (T.B.)

hacking, school riding or for dressage competitions. And since all the work, irrespective of the ultimate purpose of the horse, comes within the literal meaning of the term dressage, the book will, for the sake of simplicity, speak throughout in dressage terms. The horse to be trained will, for the same reason, be thought and spoken of as one that might ultimately graduate into the sphere of advanced dressage, notwithstanding the fact that the stages of training covered would be exactly the same for horses destined for other spheres.

The field to be covered will extend from the first lungeing lesson to the moment when the rider is confident that he could display the results of his labours with credit to both parties in a Medium dressage test. The optimum time allotted for the programme will be twenty-four months.

Introduction

The number of people who ride horses for pleasure is possibly greater today than it has ever been, and the proportion who now try, or would like to try, to train their own mounts up to a comparatively high standard of suppleness, lightness and general rideability is almost certainly much higher than it has ever been in the past. But although the ambition is there, the success rate in Great Britain is not high, the chief cause being the absence of any longstanding tradition that such work is worthwhile and the consequent scarcity of facilities for acquiring the necessary knowledge and experience.

The author believes that much better progress could be made by the average rider who works mainly on his own, without elaborate or expensive facilities, if he were better informed about what is actually practicable and what target he could reasonably set for himself and his horse. This book is intended to go some way to covering that need. It will deal in detail with a strictly limited period of training: the first two years, that being the period in which it should be possible, with very few exceptions, to endow a riding horse with all the essential qualifications for that title. He should by then be comfortable and easy to ride, and if he is not it will be the rider rather than the horse that is to blame.

The standard of education that should be expected of almost any pleasure horse worth the name will correspond to what is referred to in dressage parlance as Medium, and this should be attainable by any rider who regards himself as a reasonably proficient horseman. It involves nothing that is very difficult for a horse of average physique, conformation and temperament or for a rider of average ability and with sufficient interest to make the appropriate effort in terms of consistent study. No good horseman, once he has experienced this standard will ever again be satisfied with anything less for his hack, his hunter or his jumper. In every case the horse will perform the better for it and give infinitely greater pleasure. It should be regarded as the natural target for the all-purpose horse and the end of the first stage for the dressage specialist.

It is no accident that Medium dressage is required for the three-day event competition, that great test of the all-purpose riding horse. In the simplest terms it demands only that the horse shall stop and start; shall proceed in any direction, including sideways, in any of the three normal paces; shall carry himself and his rider in comfort and without unnecessary effort or fatigue; and shall do all these things without fuss or protest. This level of training is sadly all too seldom achieved, as may be clearly seen in many fields of equestrian activity.

PART I

General Principles

A horse of sound conformation and great strength. Peter Jones, 16.3 hands.

CHAPTER ONE

The Horse

Age

Ideally, the horse to be trained will have been handled from birth but not backed, broken or otherwise worked on. He will be between three and four years old and of sound and well-developed physique and conformation. His breeding is immaterial beyond the hope that he will not have inherited any vices or unpleasant habits.

Inevitably, many riders, by force of circumstances, will have to start work on a horse that has already been backed and may already have received quite a lot of good or bad tuition. In nearly every such case, unless the progress already made is considerable and is known to be really sound, the new owner will be well advised to follow exactly the same procedure recommended for the unbroken horse, making only the obvious adjustments to the part of the programme connected with backing, and probably shortening, but certainly not cutting out, the lungeing period. Everything else should be dealt with in the same sequence, although some of the earlier work will doubtless progress rather more quickly and more smoothly with the older and more experienced animal. But even so, the time spent on taking the new horse back through the nursery-school stages of his education will almost always pay off, not least because it enables the horse and the trainer to come to terms with and to understand each other in the easiest and pleasantest way. There are few things in equitation more helpful for psychological studies than a lunge-line – from either end of it.

On the other hand, the new owner may find that he has to deal with a handful of small but frustrating problems that originate from previous training errors that are more or less deep-seated, and which may even delay or prolong the programme he would have maintained with an unworked pupil. He would certainly be wise to ignore virtually all work supposed to have been done on any horse that has not yet reached his fourth birthday and to put him through the entire programme as though he were hitherto untouched. He will then discover many valuable pieces of information about his horse – his character, his bad habits and good points, and his general life-style – all of which will be more readily appreciated from the end of the lunge than from the more restricted and possibly slightly unsafe viewpoint of the saddle. The temptation to get on and ride the new acquisition at once, just because he has already been ridden by someone else, should be strongly resisted by a trainer who means to start right and to do the job well. Time and trouble will be saved in the long run by this more thoughtful approach.

Type of horse

Every would-be trainer has to face up to the question of what type of horse he wants or is willing to pay for and start work on. It is a long and fairly arduous undertaking, and it is important that the trainer should be content with the animal he chooses. A great deal has been written on this complicated subject, and it is not proposed to enter into it to any great extent here. Nevertheless, a quick look at some of the overriding problems will help us to start properly, and to avoid subsequent disappointments.

We should remember that a quality riding horse needs, to a greater or lesser extent, to be an athlete, and that any athlete must be strong, well proportioned and active. It is often said of a dressage horse that temperament is more important than conformation, but that is probably oversimplifying the matter. If temperament involves coolheadedness and a willingness to undertake arduous training, it is certainly vital to any athlete. But so is sound conformation, without which the body will be unable to support the stresses and strains that the work will impose on it. What is not so important is appearance. Everyone enjoys owning or just looking at a beautiful horse, but good looks seem to wilt and disappear when action fails, whereas lack of conventional good looks counts for nothing at all when the action is impressive.

As a nation we are proud of our Thoroughbred horses, but there is no evidence that they make better dressage horses than part or cross-bred animals. At the time this book is being written there is only one English Thoroughbred among the top twenty international competitors, and not many more in the top fifty. Thoroughbred blood is used extensively to improve many continental breeds, but wealthy buyers looking for dressage horses seldom look among our Thoroughbred studs. And to drive home the point that the glamour of good looks should not be overstressed, the 1976 Olympic gold medallist was one of the least conventionally good-looking horses in the business.

Many books have been written about the points to look for when buying a horse, so we will only consider here a few of those that more particularly affect the selection of a horse that may later on be required to undertake advanced dressage work.

In this context, we should pay special attention to the following considerations:

Strength in the back, behind the saddle. The horse will be asked to learn to carry himself and his rider for quite long periods in a manner that is somewhat at variance with his normal and natural way, and the physical or muscular effort required to do that is made largely by the back. Any tendency for the back to dip immediately in front of the croup should be regarded with suspicion. That is the part where the horse can most easily bend his back, and it needs to bend the other way when he lowers his quarters in collection.

Good hocks, in the right position in relation to the quarters. The hocks play a major part in all the more difficult things that the horse will be required to do. If they are not correctly placed in the first instance, under rather than slightly behind the quarters, they will be unable to play their part without grave difficulty and strain. No amount of training can positively correct the weakness caused by a faulty natural position of the hocks. It can only make the best of a bad job.

Soundness. It is a dangerous and probably expensive mistake to think that a horse that is not sound enough for other seemingly rougher pursuits will do well enough for dressage. For one thing, he will be ridden more or less the whole year round. He will need to have perfect confidence in the efficiency of his limbs, muscles and tendons, and he will make poor progress if his education is frequently interrupted by illness.

Athletic symmetry, or balance of the main parts of the body. A horse that is not naturally well balanced will be difficult to keep in balance when carrying a rider and when performing athletic exercises. In particular, the neck should flow strongly and purposefully out of the top of the withers, indicating that the forehand will assist rather than hinder the efforts of the hind quarters to lighten it. The head should not appear excessively large, and the neck should be proportionately strong enough to carry it.

Temperament, which includes courage. A good riding or dressage horse must consistently display a willingness and an anxiety to go forwards, even when under restraint or stress. He must not become over-anxious or over-excited by difficulties, and he must be willing to go on trying for long periods. For these reasons, a horse that has shown himself to be chicken-hearted across country is likely to be unsatisfactory for anything more than the lower levels of dressage. It is of course very difficult to assess these qualities in a horse that may in other respects appear quite suitable for our purpose, but a little can be guessed from the breeding, the look in the eye and the manners in the stable. The reality will appear all too clearly later on as work progresses. In the meantime, it is best to avoid an animal that appears strongly introvert in his character, and beware of that pronounced bump in the profile between the eyes that all too often denotes a thoroughly awkward or wilful outlook.

In competition on a borrowed horse in Switzerland. The author on Grant.

CHAPTER TWO

The Rider

The next thing that our would-be trainer should consider very carefully are his own qualifications for the job he is undertaking. He is going to enter into a partnership in which he will be the senior or controlling member. He must do all the planning and the thinking. He must know and set the standards. He must know in every detail precisely how to do what he wants to do at all stages; of equal importance, he must know how to relate the work he is doing at the moment to the work that will follow it. He must constantly maintain a clear vision of the whole picture and not be blinkered by the work of today. He has to obtain and maintain the co-operation of a very large animal with whom he shares no common language, whose mind will frequently and quite naturally tend to be elsewhere, and who has no means of understanding the purpose or the logic of the programme in which he will be expected to play a very active part.

These are sobering thoughts which embody such a multitude of problems and risks that it would be irresponsible for the trainer to start without taking whatever steps may be called for to ensure that he is competent to fulfil his obligations to his partner. They are the obligations of any teacher to his pupil, but with the unusual complication in this case that each and every lesson can only be taught by the doing of it. Nothing can be explained in advance. And to add the final complication, the teacher's very presence as a rider is in some ways more of a liability than an asset to the horse.

It follows clearly that the trainer, if he is to have a real chance of doing a successful job, must ensure that he starts off with a thorough knowledge of the whole project ahead of him. He also must have weighed up in his mind the main problems that are likely to arise and how they can best be dealt with. He can do this by reading, by talking to more experienced people, and by taking supervised lessons. Just as important, he must check on his own degree of polish and proficiency as a rider so that he will be able to execute his share of the proceedings without in any way hindering the obliging efforts of the horse to perform, and thereby to learn, the scheduled lessons. The smallest deviation from the correct classical principles of riding and of the application of the aids – by hand, leg, weight and seat – will inevitably and adversely affect his horse's ability to do what is asked of him in the expected manner and form. Obviously, therefore, it is absolutely essential for the trainer to ride correctly, and to take lessons to achieve that aim if he is not confident about himself, before he can hope to train a horse correctly. Of course, many people will have a go despite their self-acknowledged deficiencies as horsemen, and quite rightly in many cases, but at least they should know the theory, be humble enough to recognize the dangers, and strive with all their ability to improve as they go along.

Ideally, every rider should first learn, by working on a trained horse, each and every lesson that he wishes to teach his pupil. In practice that may not always be possible, especially in the United Kingdom where there are hardly any riding schools that maintain horses capable of being ridden through all the standard movements. In that case the novice trainer should make great efforts to have an hour or so of talk and discussion with a good and experienced rider before he tackles any new lesson on his own.

In this context it is supremely important that the trainer should be quite certain that his own body and limbs are as fit and supple as he wishes those of his horse to be. The horse world is full of people who talk about the suppleness, or lack of suppleness, of their own or other people's horses, but it is remarkable how seldom the suppleness of the rider is mentioned or questioned. Yet a stiff rider will never make a supple horse, and it is quite true that a stiff rider will quickly ruin a horse that was once supple. Strictly speaking, and in fairness to the horses, no rider who does not have a supple back and limbs should try to train a young horse. And indeed there is no reason why he should because there is no excuse whatever for the normal young or middle-aged rider to be stiff. To achieve and maintain an adequate degree of suppleness should be as normal and as integral a part of his attitude to equitation as cleaning his boots, perhaps more so. All that is necessary is a few minutes of daily bending and stretching exercises. That, particularly for those over thirty, is the first essential.

Next, in logical sequence, is a course of lessons on a lunge-horse from someone who knows the business, followed by occasional refresher lessons of the same sort. And any feeling of humiliation that such a thing should be thought necessary for 'me' can be quickly smoothed away by the knowledge that many of the greatest riders in the world consider it worthwhile to have themselves lunged at very regular intervals. To sum this problem up, you cannot teach what you don't know, and you cannot teach anything well unless your teaching tools, which in this case are your body and limbs, are fit for the job.

All dressage, whether competitive or otherwise, is a combined effort in which the rider, being the thinking partner, must give at least as much attention to his own performance as to that of his other half. The two performances are inextricably interlocked and interdependent, and the rider, being the leader, will need to carry on a perpetual running check-up of the key points of his techniques, as if he were watching himself in a mirror with a shrewd and critical eye.

A paragraph in the FEI *Rules for Dressage* lays down clearly and precisely all the requirements of the correct and classical seat, and then adds: 'This is the only position making it possible for the rider to school the horse progressively and correctly.' That short and simple-sounding statement, together with the list of requirements that precede it, should be taken quite literally, pondered over and never forgotten.

All the movements should be obtained without apparent effort of the rider. He should be well balanced with his loins and hips supple, thighs and legs steady and well stretched downwards. The upper part of the body easy, free and erect, with hands low and close together without, however, touching either each other or the horse and with the thumb as the highest point; the elbows and arms close to the body, enabling the rider to follow the movements of the horse smoothly and freely and to apply his aids imperceptibly.★

Such is the essence of classical riding, distilled from generations of thought and practical study. Those simple and weighty words contain all that it is necessary to know, and yet their full implications are difficult to comprehend without prolonged thought. The rider who has never had, or cannot continue to have, lessons from a top-class riding master should try to memorize them. He may also find it helpful to check himself frequently against the following notes on some of the key points that are embodied in the official summary and which will, for better or worse, affect his progress as a trainer.

★FEI *Rules for Dressage*, Article 417 (14th Edition)

The head must be held high above the shoulders so that its very considerable weight flows straight down through the spine. Any displacement of the head, forwards, backwards or sideways, will significantly and adversely affect the rider's, and consequently also the horse's, balance. This factor becomes increasingly important as the training progresses. As the horse is asked to execute more and more difficult exercises the nicety of the balance becomes more acute. The carriage of the rider's head, which weighs between ten and fourteen pounds, will also affect the carriage and action of the rider's torso which itself directly governs his influence on the horse.

The upper part of the body must be 'free, easy and erect' with the weight flowing straight down through the seat bones into the heels. The word erect is important and can be interpreted as meaning that the rider should not only sit vertically above his seat bones but should feel as tall as possible with the caution that in doing so he must not become stiff and in particular must maintain the suppleness of the small of the back and of his loins and hips. It is not as easy as it may sound at first to combine the qualities demanded by those three simple words – free, easy and erect – but their effective importance is as great as anything else in riding and deserves intense study and thought by all riders.

In no circumstances should the shoulders be in front of the vertical so that they precede the seat in following the movement of the horse. If that happens some of the rider's weight is removed from the seat bones, and he can no longer influence his horse correctly and effectively.

The lower part of the spine or small of the back, together with the hips and loins, plays a crucial part in the relationship between horse and rider. This is the part of the spine that absorbs the bumps that would otherwise make the trot, and even the canter, quite uncomfortable to sit through. Fortunately the human spine was designed almost ideally for sitting comfortably on a horse, provided the rider learns to utilize nature's conformation to the best advantage. The spine has a natural and definite forward bend in the region between the lower ribs and the pelvis (Fig. 1a). This is also the part of the spine that is most flexible. It is that natural forward bend that must be kept supple and utilized so that it can act as a shock-absorber when the weight of the body comes down into the saddle; for example, at the end of each sitting-trot stride, just at the moment when the saddle is beginning to rise again as the horse pushes himself off the ground for the next stride. There is no way in which the rider can escape the purely mechanical fact that it is the horse that dictates the direction and timing of each and every movement up or down

Figure 1   *The mechanics and the influence of the seat*

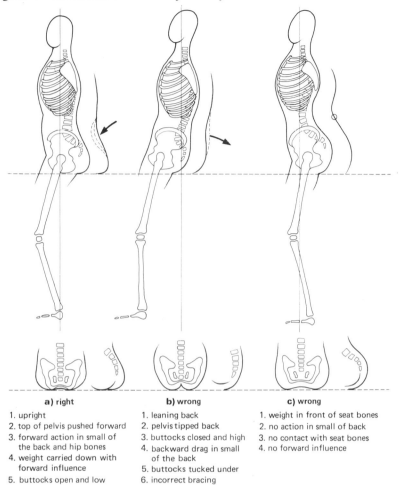

a) right

1. upright
2. top of pelvis pushed forward
3. forward action in small of the back and hip bones
4. weight carried down with forward influence
5. buttocks open and low
6. lower spine effective as shock-absorber

b) wrong

1. leaning back
2. pelvis tipped back
3. buttocks closed and high
4. backward drag in small of the back
5. buttocks tucked under
6. incorrect bracing
7. no forward influence
8. spine unable to act as shock-absorber

c) wrong

1. weight in front of seat bones
2. no action in small of back
3. no contact with seat bones
4. no forward influence

and that there must inevitably be a tiny time-lag in which the rider's body has to accommodate itself to the changes of movement and to the bumps created by inertia and gravity. Because the bumps inconvenience the horse, and the rider too for that matter, they must be absorbed as much as possible, and this is done by allowing the spine, in the area of the small of the back, to flex forward a trifle beyond its normal stationary form, just for an instant before it again reflexes back to the normal. There is, of course, no actual pause between the flexion and reflexion which flow smoothly into each other with absolute regularity so long as the horse's pace continues at the same speed. The greater the vertical move-ment of the horse, the more supple will the small of the back have to be to absorb the movement without an unsightly, uncomfortable and rhythm-destroying bump.

It should not be thought that the sitting trot is the only pace at which the suppleness of the small of the back is required. It operates to a greater or lesser degree at all paces in which the rider is sitting in the saddle as opposed to standing in the stirrups, not excluding the walk. But the problem is most acute in the sitting trot and will vary in degree accord-ing to the conformation and athleticism of the individual horse as well as to the elevation and length of stride. The stresses placed on the rider's back are far greater, for example, in a passage – which is a very elevated trot – or in an extended trot – which is both lengthened and elevated – than in a normal working or collected trot.

The degree to which the spine flexes within these extremes has to be controlled and adjusted by the muscles in that area of the back. To achieve that control, the rider must learn to increase or decrease the tension in those muscles according to the requirements of the moment including the degree of influence he wishes his back to exert on the horse. For example, when he increases the muscle tension, he proportionately decreases the degree of forward flexion of the spine and, in doing so, increases the influence of his weight on the seat bones. This increase in muscle tension is, in effect, what is more conventionally known as bracing the back. When the rider decreases the muscle tension, he inevitably increases the freedom of the spine to flex, the shock-absorber works more effectively, the horse is less conscious of the weight on the seat bones, and the influence of the rider's seat is less powerful. But always, no matter how much bracing is applied, some degree of supple-ness and flexibility of the spine must be retained, though under greater or lesser tension according to circumstances.

The regular and recurrent forward supple flexion of the small of the back, present to a greater or lesser extent in all paces, allows the rider to remain constantly in soft, quiet and unbroken contact with the saddle and so with the horse's back. But that flexion also has the almost equally important effect of carrying the main weight of the rider's body a little bit forward with the movement of the horse so that he is truly 'following the movement', and also, because the main weight lies above the point of flexion, a little bit also downward and closer to the saddle.

If the rider fails to develop the correct action of the back in this manner, one of two things will result, both of them disastrous to the progress of the horse. If the back is not supple, he consequently has no shock-absorbing flexion or 'ripple', he will bump the horse's back at every trot stride and eventually ruin it, together with all hope of ever achieving a cadenced rhythm. Alternatively, the rider will instinctively endeavour to soften the bump by trying to use a backward ripple of his spine. In effect he collapses the small of his back (see Fig 1b). This latter action is contrary to the natural shape of the spine; it is against the forward movement of the horse; it puts the weight towards the back of the saddle where it is not wanted; it allows the shoulders and the head to collapse; it adversely and directly affects the ability of the hands to follow and encourage the forward movement; and is altogether deplorable. The correct forward 'ripple', on the other hand, directly assists the rider in avoiding each and every one of those pitfalls. It should also be appreciated that the forward and downward action causes the seat bones to exert a driving influence on the horse because they, and the whole pelvis, are carried forward by the flexing spine. The greater the muscle tension, the stronger the drive, provided only that the muscles remain supple.

The author has heard it said that any forward ripple in the small of the back tends to make the rider adopt the undesirable crutch seat (see Fig. 1c). There is, however, no danger of this happening provided that the flexion takes place under a degree of tension and consequently reflexes back still under tension to the normal upright position each time, and provided also that the pelvis always precedes the shoulders. Certainly if the spine is flexed and then held with stiff muscles in the fully flexed position, the rider will indeed be in the crutch position because the pelvis, which is attached to the spine, will have rocked forward a fraction on the seat bones according to the degree of flexion of the spine. But the degree of rock is in any case infinitesimal and is of no consequence provided that it is not static and the head and shoulders remain erect.

In case the reader is still not clear about the correct action of the back, which has been described in some detail because of its importance, it may help if we borrow an explanation used by Mrs Hublon in her book on side-saddle riding. If you balance a broomstick upright on the end of a diving board and then activate the diving board, the broomstick will bounce. If you replace the broomstick with a piece of rope, placing one end of the rope on the board and holding the other in the air, the rope-end will remain comfortably on the board when the latter is activated . . . because it is supple and capable of rippling. The rider must learn to emulate the rope and not the broomstick, remembering only that his spine has by nature been predisposed to rippling in the forward direction.

The hands should remain at all times so as to form an absolutely straight line between the bit and the rider's elbow. Any suggestion that it can in some circumstances be helpful to keep the hands below that straight line should be discounted entirely and its practice regarded as one of the deadly sins of riding. No other single fault in riding is so certain to spoil and even ruin a horse's paces than hands that are held too low. Too low means, in effect, down at the level of, or even touching, the withers. In that position they invariably become, together with the forearm and elbow, a little set and stiff, and that sets up a counter resistance by the horse. At the very least the horse will be aware that the hands are not generous, with the result that he will be reluctant to go boldly forward to the bit and will get into the way of staying just behind it. He will consequently never develop the vitalizing impulsion that flows forward through the back to the mouth and back to the hands. He will quite soon become flat and stiff in his back, which makes riding very uncomfortable.

It is a sad fact that there are some instructors and riding schools that actually teach the altogether deplorable habit of low-positioned hands. Sometimes it is said that it is a help to the rider in his efforts to keep his hands still, apparently forgetting that the horse's head has to move according to the pace and to the forward flow of muscular action and so the hands have to move accordingly. It is sometimes suggested that low hands help to counteract a tendency for the horse to carry his head, or his nose, too high. That is an entirely fallacious theory and ignores the basic fact that all horses tend by nature to pull away from any discomfort or pain. So in practice the low, stiff and resisting hand is likely to cause the horse to adopt a high, resistant headcarriage with a consequent and fatal hollowing of his back. The desired lowering of the head into a natural and comfortable position is more likely to be achieved by raising the hands, if necessary quite high, where they can at least be sensitive and will also encourage the horse to take the bit in the opposite direction which in this case will be downwards.

But when all is said and done, the best and most helpful position is one in which the hands are well clear of the withers and always in that straight line with the mouth. The exact height will naturally vary just a little according to the height at which the horse is carrying his head, but the variation will in practice be so small as to be negligible.

The legs should hang down so that they maintain a constant, light and relaxed contact with the horse from the seat bones as far down towards the ankle as possible, with their own weight flowing uninterruptedly into the heel. It is more important to have contact with the lower part of the calf than the knees. There should be no sensation of any form of grip at any point of the legs, thus leaving them quite free for their job of feeling, communicating and creating impulsion. They should be as relaxed and as gentle as the hands, arms and shoulders, so that they can carry on a continuous conversation with the horse, alternately listening and replying. They should never move from their 'home' position on the girth, with the heels just behind the girth, except when one or the other is deliberately moved to a slightly different position in order to call for some specific action or reaction from the horse.

The rider should practise a very high degree of accurate and consistent placing of his legs. In that way the horse, being a creature of habit, quickly learns to listen and to respond with equal accuracy. In order to develop this talkative stillness of the legs, which increases the horse's confidence as well as his attention, the rider should remember that his legs should seldom, if ever, move backward from their position on the girth except only when he wishes to influence the lateral movement of the quarters. All signals calling for forward movement of any kind are given on the girth, if necessary with a very slight forward action, against the grain of the hair. The horse is far less sensitive on the wider part of his rib-cage, and to use the legs in a backward direction in order to induce horse to go forward is psychologically inept. In so far as such wrong aids do produce some reaction, it is mainly from a combination of brute force on the part of the rider and discomfort on the part of the horse. They have no place in the vocabulary of fine horsemanship. This important matter of the correct and most effective use of the rider's legs is discussed in more detail later on.

CHAPTER THREE

Time Factor and Working Conditions

Time

So far, then, we have discussed the preparedness and qualifications of the rider to undertake the education of a young horse. We have also concluded that it is not difficult to find a perfectly suitable young animal to be trained into a thoroughly satisfactory riding horse with some potential for other more specialized or more active roles. During the process of training, there will also be a great deal of learning and enjoyment. But there are two further factors to be looked into, the importance of which should not be underestimated. These are the availability of time and of space in which the work will be carried out. To achieve our object, the trainer must be able to allocate approximately one hour a day, for at least five days a week, to the task. Time off for the occasional short holiday of two or three weeks for the benefit of both horse and trainer is recommended, but for routine purposes a disciplined regularity of work is virtually essential. Almost nothing of value will be achieved, for instance, by someone whose available time is limited to weekends, or to a few irregular days in each week. In any case there will be interruptions for domestic emergencies and minor veterinary problems. On the other hand, a maximum of one hour a day will suffice, and very often even less will be required, particularly in the early stages. Indeed, throughout the training, and bearing in mind the prime necessity for keeping the horse fresh and interested, the rider would be well advised to aim at doing forty-five minutes' good work, with sixty minutes' work only on rare

Bending and suppling on a circle. The author on Peter Jones.

occasions. These times do not take account of the normal stable routine, nor of the time required to travel to and from the working area.

Working conditions

Because the young horse will have to be worked regularly, in all seasons and in nearly all weather, the availability of suitable riding space becomes paramount. Access to a covered manège solves all the most obvious problems in this respect, though it is not necessarily ideal as the sole place to work and is certainly not essential. Excellent results can be obtained from any open, flat, reasonably smooth and well-drained grass area, though a minimum of about two acres is needed if it is to survive constant use. Much will depend on the nature of the top- and subsoil, the speed of recovery after heavy rain or a spell of prolonged wet weather, and whether or not the trainer enjoys sole use and control over the area. Working a horse on slippery or badly poached ground will do more harm than good as it spoils the horse's confidence in his stride and balance.

There are various compromises between the covered school and the more or less unrestricted open area. An open, all-weather manège is useful and can be essential if the available grass area is not flat, but it is expensive to construct and will need quite a lot of laborious maintenance to keep it in good condition. Given the choice between a really good well-drained paddock and a single manège without any additional work area, the author would quite definitely choose the former, which carries with it, among other benefits, a greater scope for variety and less risk of boredom.

Nevertheless, the trainer who has to work without the advantages of either a covered school or an all-weather manège does have to face the serious problem of how and where to carry through his lungeing work. Correct lungeing on a circle damages the grass land. If the ground is at all wet it will very quickly become badly poached and take a long time to recover. In such circumstances it can also be harmful and even damaging to the horse. It must therefore be realized that, even in the best conditions of grass and soil, a serious lungeing programme is not a practical proposition for under two acres.

The trainer faced with this problem can do one of two things. If he has access to ample land, he can so arrange things that he starts work on his young horse in the late spring when he can at least hope to have three fairly dry months for his lunge work. By choosing the best ground and by frequently changing his pitch, he can hopefully avoid the main troubles. Alternatively, and very much to be recommended, he can try to find the small area and the relatively small amount of money, probably between £100 and £200, required to construct an all-weather permanent lunge-ring. He will find such a ring quite invaluable both in the short and the long run. To begin with, it will allow him to take his horse through the all-important lungeing phase of his training under ideal conditions; it will be available for use whenever the weather or other factors such as illness or business pressures make it inconvenient for him to ride; and it will be available whenever a change in the daily routine seems advisable to assist in warding off staleness or to assess development.

A lunge-ring should be from fourteen to sixteen metres in diameter, and it must have good natural or induced drainage. Allowance will have to be made for the fact that the circular perimeter track will receive a very heavy pounding which must not be permitted to penetrate right through the surface dressing to the subsoil, at any rate if the latter is clay. Expert advice should be taken as to how best to treat the working surface and also as to what type or types of sub-surface should be laid over the subsoil. All this will vary according to the site, the soil, the slope and the amount of work it will be required to carry. For instance, a one-horse man will probably be able to take greater risks by adopting a relatively economical prescription than someone who is likely to have a number of horses using the ring.

A perimeter edging of some strong and horse-safe material such as old railway sleepers will be necessary on most sites to maintain the overall shape, and a light rail or ring of hurdles above the edging is a not too expensive luxury that has its advantages in assisting to maintain the pupil's attention and in preventing unauthorized exit or entry.

Attentive, active and light on the aids. Dr Reiner Klimke on Notturno.

CHAPTER FOUR

Principles of Lungeing

Lungeing means working the young horse on a lunge-rein without a rider, and a full three months has been allotted to this work. At first sight this may seem a very long time to devote to dismounted work, and many people are tempted to cut it short and to start riding much earlier than this programme recommends. Some even advocate that the young horse should be mounted as soon as he is quiet enough to be moderately safe so that the trainer can 'master' him before he becomes too strong. The latter policy is a sad reflection on the trainer's understanding of equine psychology and physiology as well as on his confidence in his own horsemanship. The only time, in fact, that it would be wiser to cut short the lungeing time is if the lunge-ground were to become so cut up that it was unsafe and unprofitable to continue the work.

There is a great deal to do and to be achieved in the lunge period, and if the work is done thoroughly the time allowed will be none too long. Every minute that is well spent on the lunge will pay a big dividend throughout the remainder of the training.

The daily work will gradually extend, as the horse gets fitter, from an initial ten or fifteen minutes to an ultimate maximum of forty or forty-five minutes. Gradually we shall demand more and more positive activity, more and more immediate but smooth response and obedience to our commands.

Lungeing tack

Before we can set about this exciting task of creating, literally in our hand, a calm, strong, obedient, powerful and active horse, we must be sure that we have the correct lungeing tack and the knowledge of how it should be used. There are a few people who are able to produce remarkably good results on the lunge by more or less unconventional methods or with tack that would normally be regarded as less than adequate. But such people possess an abnormal degree of talent, amounting to genius, which cannot be emulated by the average trainer.

The essential requirements for correct lungeing are:

A *snaffle bridle* of the smooth-mouthed, single-jointed type. It is important that this should fit the horse's mouth and not be too wide or too narrow in the mouthpiece. The correct fitting for any bit is that the mouthpiece itself should, when opened out, be just 1·3 centimetres (½ inch) wider between the rings than the width of the mouth as measured from the outer edges of the lips by passing a stick or footrule through the mouth. In other words, there should be no more than a half a centimetre (¼ inch) between the lips and the rings of the snaffle on each side when the bit is fully extended. If the snaffle is too wide there is a likelihood of it being pulled too far to one side, with the result that the joint in the mouthpiece is no longer in the centre of the mouth and may even be pressing right on one of the bars. Not only is this liable to hurt and damage the bars, it will also restrict the freedom of the tongue normally provided for by the angle formed in the mouthpiece when the reins are taut. There can be few things more likely to cause mouth troubles than an ill-fitting bit.

Quite a wide variety of snaffle bits, jointed, double-jointed or unjointed, are available and indeed used, and the inexperienced rider may find this confusing and will probably be tempted to experiment with some or all of them in an effort to solve real or merely anticipated or imaginary problems with his horse. In the big majority of cases it is wisest to start with and to stick to the simple, loose-ringed, thick-mouthpieced, single-jointed snaffle commonly known as the German snaffle. There are a few cases where a different style of bit will or may help a horse with a difficult or fussy mouth, but all too frequently the hoped-for advantages or improvements turn out after a few days' trial to be largely illusory. A lot of money can all too easily be spent and wasted on such experiments, and it is more profitable to pin one's faith on the principle that a horse will give of his best when he is happy and not unnecessarily burdened. He will be more sensitive to his bit than to any other part of his equipment, and that item should therefore be light, simple and gentle of action. For regular lungeing work the author recommends the use of a suitable snaffle bit attached only to a simple headstall, without browband, noseband, throatlatch or reins. This simple convenience considerably reduces the daily bridling and unbridling chore and makes it easier to fit the somewhat cumbersome cavesson, besides reducing to a minimum the amount of overall clutter on the horse's head.

A *roller*, or alternatively a surcingle to be worn over a saddle, with two or three metal rings or 'd's sewn to the front edge on both sides, and one centrally placed at the back. A roller is certainly preferable to the surcingle and saddle in the early days with a young and possibly nervous animal, as well as being very much lighter and easier to handle.

A *cavesson headcollar* which, in effect, is an extra-strong leather headstall with a padded and reinforced noseband and a low-fitting and strong throatlatch. The noseband is fitted tightly though not uncomfortably either just above or just below the bit. In the latter case it must be high enough so as not to interfere with the horse's breathing or bear on the sensitive lower parts of the muzzle. With the lunge-rein attached to the front ring of the cavesson noseband, virtually any horse, however strong or wild, can be controlled without pulling on or risking damage to his mouth. Throughout the training, no trouble should be spared to maintain the natural and original sensitivity of the mouth, and it is for this reason advisable and worthwhile to use the cavesson whenever the young horse is being led outside his stable. Without it, any sudden nervousness or youthful vivacity will probably be countered by overpowerful and hurtful pulls on the snaffle which may do at least slight but irreparable harm to the immature mouth.

Leather side reins, preferably with easy-release clips for attachment to the rings of the snaffle, and with buckle adjustment for length at one or both ends. A minimum adjustment of ten holes will be essential and more may be required, depending on the make and shape of the horse. The use of elastic inserts in side reins is to be strongly deprecated as some horses learn to play with them, making them stretch and contract. This playing with the reins can easily become a bad habit which will eventually have to be eradicated, and will in any case interfere with the work and distract the horse's attention. Very short elastic inserts, not more than fifteen centimetres in length, that shorten but do not cause a break in the leather may be acceptable though they serve little purpose beyond providing the trainer with a visual check on the amount of pressure being exerted on the reins. The inexperienced trainer will probably be surprised to find that the pressure exerted by the horse is virtually never enough to straighten out the leather loop formed by the insert.

It is very important that the trainer should be clear in his mind about the purpose and advantages of using side reins for all lungeing work. They play a vital role, and there are six main reasons for their use:

1.   They provide the trainer with a simple but remarkably effective method of controlling the natural waywardness and inattention of most young horses. They make it difficult, if not actually impossible, for the horse to turn his neck away from his line of progression, and they limit the extent to which he can throw his head up or down. Because they are quite firmly anchored to the roller and therefore have no pulling effect of any kind, no horse will pull against them or fight them. They therefore cannot harm the mouth, and they tend to exercise a valuable calming influence.

2.   By the mere weight of the reins, they help to keep the bit still in the mouth and discourage excessive playing with it.

3.   The horse learns from them to accept a light contact with the bit without being afraid of it, exactly as will be required when we come to ride him with ordinary reins. This contact through the side reins will increase and improve as his impulsion increases and as the side reins are gradually shortened in accordance with the development of his self-carriage.

4.   They enable the trainer to teach the horse to search forward for his bit by lengthening his neck. It is not entirely clear why horses will do this, though it may be that they prefer, once they are really working, to use the steadying and balancing effect of contact. Whatever the explanation, which is probably more psychological than physical, it is a very valuable lesson that must be worked for from the outset and always maintained throughout all future work. Perhaps its greatest value is that it helps to keep the horse's back unrestricted and free for the passage of the muscular waves that flow from the quarters to the forehand and mouth. Conversely, a tendency to shorten the neck results in a more or less stiff back that restricts the paces and is uncomfortable to sit on.

5.   They encourage balanced self-carriage. Little by little though never to the point of restriction, the side reins are shortened so that, taking advantage of the fact that the horse will never pull or lean on them if he can avoid it, the trainer can gradually impose a shortened frame within which the horse has to work. But this process must be very gradual and never pushed faster than the development of the horse's muscular elasticity will allow. Thus the horse learns, without the weight of a rider on his back, to carry himself in a more upright and proud outline with his own weight less and less on his forehand, steadily developing in the

process the muscles that he will eventually require to carry his rider equally proudly, but always with a supple, stretching and pulsating back and neck.

6.   They provide, in conjunction with the lunge-rein and the whip, a means by which the trainer can begin to teach collection. It would be virtually impossible to do this without the restraining and the straightening effect of side reins.

Without doubt there are a few people who can achieve high standards of work on the lunge without side reins, but for the average, or even above average, trainer they are a necessity for anything approaching the full potentialities of lunge training. Without them only a very modest and incomplete achievement is practicable. With them, lunge work can be carried to almost unlimited heights and certainly to the point where it overlaps, and so eases and shortens, the first six months or more of mounted work. Unless they are used with an unusual lack of care and intelligence they can at worst do no harm and must do at least some good.

Lungeing whip. The use and purpose of this vital piece of equipment would appear to be inadequately understood if one is to judge by the standard of whips seen in the tack rooms of many people who train horses. It is just as important that it should be of good quality and correct proportions as any other piece of equipment, or else the training will suffer. The whip is needed either to exercise an indirect and moral influence on the behaviour of the horse or a direct and tangible influence by its ability to touch the horse on carefully selected parts of its anatomy. But in neither case must it ever be used so as to frighten nor to cause anxiety by implying that it might be used to hurt. The horse must be brought up from the beginning to accept the whip as a friendly necessity within the educational process, although admittedly there will be an unspoken assumption between pupil and trainer that the whip could hurt a little if it were ever used in that way. But that acknowledgement should never be put to the test for fear of breaking the friendship. It follows that if the whip is to maintain its proper influence the horse must be aware that he can be touched with it. For that to be done with accuracy and timing, it is obviously essential that the overall length of the whip, from the butt to the tip of the lash, must be approximately the same as the longest length of lunge-rein likely to be used. Any whip that is shorter than the lunge-rein becomes nothing but an empty threat, and the trainer will be unable to exert any influence with it except by swishing it through the air in an undesirably threatening manner that is bound to disturb the horse's mental and physical equilibrium. If the whip is too long or too heavy it will be difficult to handle delicately and accurately, and may be very tiring to the wrist.

In addition to being the correct length, it should also be light and well balanced. The trainer should aim to handle his whip with the same degree of accuracy as a dry-fly fisherman his fly. In both cases a coarse instrument will make accuracy nearly impossible.

Boots, to protect the inside of the cannon bone, the tendons and the fetlock joint should always be worn when lungeing which inevitably involves some risk of damage from the strain and fatigue implicit in continuous work on a circle.

A *crupper* may be necessary in exceptional cases, as with a horse in very poor condition or of weak conformation, to prevent the roller from being pulled forward by the side reins, though this is very unlikely as has already been shown when discussing the side reins.

Purpose of lungeing

Learning to work

The first purpose of lungeing is to accustom the young horse to the business of learning to work, and like everything else we do we want to begin this first lesson in a manner that is as easy and as painless as possible. The horse will have no idea what work is all about, and he will hardly have been asked to apply his mind to anything more demanding than allowing himself to be groomed. He will therefore be soft and flabby in his muscles and in his mind; his bones will perhaps only recently have become properly set, and he will be totally unready to face the mental surprise and the physical strain of accepting a heavy human burden on his back. But sadly, the early mounting method of breaking a horse is all too frequently used, regardless of the harm it probably causes to immature muscle and mouth and the subsequent delays due to the time taken in eradicating these early but avoidable troubles. We wish to give our pupil the best possible chance right from the beginning, and to do this we must adopt a course that holds the maximum prospect of a clear run through.

Muscular development

The next important principle of a really comprehensive lungeing programme is to develop the horse's musculature, particularly in the region of his back, quarters and neck, so that in due course he will be able to carry a rider quite easily. His musculature will naturally continue to develop, but in the first instance we have to create the essential minimum of muscle where only fat has previously existed, and to develop it in the right places. That is bound to take a considerable time and quite certainly cannot be done in just one or two weeks of light lungeing.

Tendons, ligaments, heart, lungs and general condition also have to be considered and prepared for the work-life for which the horse is being trained. They all need very careful attention in this youthful stage and lungeing is the ideal way in which this attention can be given. The trainer can see the whole horse at all times and can gauge his every action and reaction. His eye never leaves his pupil, and he can watch with a detailed accuracy that can never be equalled from the saddle.

Qualities developed from lungeing

Self-carriage

We have already touched on the subject of the self-carriage that is one of the important results of lunge work on side reins and is indeed one of the chief purposes of lungeing. It carries with it the development of simple physical fitness by which we mean the growth and toning up of the whole body structure so that the horse will be able to undertake the tasks asked of him without strain or fatigue. One of those tasks is to carry a rider. But muscles can only be developed through steady and consistent work, and that work must be done in the right posture if the right muscles are to benefit. Hence the importance of correct self-carriage. Hence the fact that if a horse is allowed to do his daily stint on the lunge in a sloppy manner, without the discipline imposed by side reins, he will be doing little to develop the muscles that will eventually be required to carry himself and his rider. He will therefore be unfit when he is eventually mounted, and this in turn is likely to lead to further bad postural habits which may be difficult or even impossible to eradicate.

Dexterity

Another quality required of any riding horse, and one that can most beneficially be developed initially without the burden of a rider, is that of dexterity. By dexterity we mean the speed and ease with which the horse can adjust his balance to different circumstances, and the degree to which he is light and agile on his feet when changing direction or type of movement.

Confidence

Then there is the all-important matter of mutual confidence, and perhaps more especially the confidence of the horse in the trainer. Horses are by nature fearful, and they react very quickly to anything that they do not understand or which surprises or hurts them. Nothing useful can be done with a horse when he is frightened or when he is sufficiently alarmed to fix his attention elsewhere than on his trainer or rider.

The early establishment of confidence that the trainer will do nothing to alarm or hurt him is a prime consideration. This is something that can be achieved much more quickly in lunge work than when riding because the horse can then see the source of his unwonted control; because he can so easily be controlled without resort to pressure on the sensitive mouth which in any case he will not understand at this stage of his education; and because there is no heavy weight on his back to upset his normal balancing processes. It is this same absence of unbalance and discomfort that makes the horse more readily susceptible to absorbing lessons and to giving his attention to the point of obedience. A habit of obedience acquired on the lunge will obviate innumerable later disagreements or struggles that could cause harm to the horse's mouth or mind.

Communication

By no means the least of the many benefits to be gained from lungeing is that it enables us to establish a clearly understood language, a means of communication, between trainer and horse. It is true that the language used initially on the lunge consists mainly of the voice and the whip, neither of which will be much used in the subsequent ridden work. But the lunge-language has the advantage of being supremely simple, and also painless, with the result that it is quickly learnt, understood and obeyed. There will be no difficulty, later on, in converting the communication symbols used on the lunge into the corresponding and more directly logical symbols or aids that will have to be used from the saddle.

Calmness

A prime concern for the first few weeks on the lunge will be to establish calmness. This may have to be achieved in the first place by a degree of boredom, but calmness there must be and the trainer must use all his ingenuity and his personality to achieve it. Without it there can be no true submission, no attention, no relaxation and only a much reduced ability to learn. Later will come activity, but never at the expense of calmness.

Relaxation

Second only to calmness will be the need for the horse to relax the muscles of his back and neck and to reach forward and downward with his head when in motion. Here we are touching on something that will concern us right through the whole educational process, no matter how far that goes. It is bound up in the long run with collection which itself is at the heart of all serious equitation. Very briefly, the logic of the matter is that, in order to collect, the horse must slightly shorten his base line. To do that he must correspondingly lengthen his top line, and to do that his spine must be stretched and slightly rounded upwards. The neck must stretch forwards so that the normally somewhat sagging part of the spine that lies within the forehand or thorax can rise and so lengthen the whole column from poll to dock. The end result is to enable the quarters to lower and come further under the mass, but it all has to begin with the lengthening of the neck. And that is where we start.

The trainer should expect to lengthen or shorten the side reins two or three times during the course of a lesson, especially during the last month or so of the lunge programme when both collection and extension are being taught. These fairly frequent alterations to the length of the side reins will also help to keep the horse's neck muscles soft and pliable. They should be made in accordance with what the trainer's eyes tell him are the physical requirements of the horse when performing the movement asked of him.

Lunge training should, if possible, be programmed to include such relatively demanding transitions as walk, or even halt, to canter; canter to walk; medium trot to collected trot; and perhaps half-pirouette on the haunches. Thus the horse is taught to be attentive and agile.

A classic shoulder-in by Nuno Oliveira.

CHAPTER FIVE

Making the Programme

Well before we intend starting work on our young horse it is very important to work out in some detail the programme we intend to follow for twenty-four steady and fruitful months. We must imprint on our mind a clear vision of the goal at the end and an equally clear picture of each step. We have to take with us along that route a companion with an altogether different mentality and form of intelligence, who cannot be pushed or cajoled, but will co-operate wholeheartedly if only he is given the chance to understand what is expected of him. Our programme must therefore be worked out in terms that are simple, logical and comprehensive. Each new step must be recognizable as a logical sequel to the one before and must not be entered upon until its predecessor has been thoroughly well established.

Right from the start we must take every precaution to ensure that the horse is physically as well as mentally fit and ready for the next step before we ask him to take it. As a very simple example of this, we should not put our weight on his back until we have arranged matters so that there is sufficient muscle in that region to enable him to carry the strange new burden in comfort. We must remember that up to this point in his life he will not have developed any more muscle than was necessary to carry his own weight around the field to graze and play. He will have very little firm muscle anywhere, and virtually none in the area where we shall sit. To begin riding a young horse before some additional muscle has been put there by appropriate work is to risk doing real and serious harm to one of the most important parts of our horse's anatomy. The equivalent in human terms would be suddenly to introduce a teenage schoolboy to a course of gymnastics and at the same time to insist that he carry a fifteen-pound suitcase strapped to the small of his back. It would obviously be wiser to defer the introduction of the burdensome suitcase to some later date. The same principle of physical preparation will occur right through the training process, though never more importantly than at this early stage.

Timing the programme

The training programme, intended to cover many months of steadily progressive development, should be worked out and written down in sufficient detail to ensure that it can be remembered and adhered to. A written programme not only forces the compiler to think carefully and constructively about the whole range of the project, it also has the practical advantage that it will be available throughout the work for periodic reference and check-up, this being especially valuable for those riders who are not very experienced or are not too confident of their direction. Later, and after training a number of horses, they may be able to dispense with the written programme.

It has already been stated that two years should be sufficient to take an average horse up to the standard we have in mind. A glance at the outline work programme recommended by the author at the end of Part 1 will show that the schedule has been divided into eight three-monthly periods. This method may cause some criticism from people who are used to hearing it said that the time factor should never be allowed to influence the training of a horse. Taken quite literally, that is of course perfectly true, but to some extent it oversimplifies the matter. Certainly we must work within the principle that nothing new shall be attempted until the horse has been thoroughly prepared, both mentally and physically, in the preceding work. That rule must never be forgotten, and if the work falls behind the suggested timetable the trainer must accept it without impatience and without falling prey to the temptation to take some short-cut to catch up on the time that appears to have been lost. But by the very act of checking his progress against a reasonable schedule, his attention will have been drawn to the fact that something is not going according to plan, and he will be encouraged to look closely to discover the cause or his own weakness. He may thus learn a lesson or become aware earlier than he would otherwise have done that some alteration or adjustment to his methods is called for. For example, it is necessary though not always easy for the less experienced trainer to learn to distinguish between exercising reasonable and salutary discipline and, on the other hand, exerting potentially harmful pressure in order to obtain premature results. A check against the programme may serve to reinforce his judgement on such matters.

Again, the trainer may find that some section of the work is going particularly smoothly and is ahead of the schedule. In that case he may decide to ease up on that aspect and give correspondingly more time to working on problems that are proving more difficult or have not yet been properly established. In the author's opinion, the dangers of a written schedule for an intelligent rider are small and are far outweighed by the many advantages.

Those who tend to disagree on principle with the whole idea of setting a programme to a time scale, however provisional the time factor may be, are ignoring the fact that every experienced trainer who has done the job many times before will invariably have a perfectly clear mental picture of how long he expects to take, barring accidents or the occurrence of exceptionally difficult problems, to cover each and all of the main stages of a basic training programme such as we are considering. So let us not be afraid of a timed programme. There will be a very great deal to be done before we have finished the job, and it will not be easy to keep a clear view of all the links in the chain of events without some help of this kind.

Sequence of the programme

The programme is designed primarily to show the sequence in which the many different aspects of the work should, in the best interests of the horse's education and development, be introduced into the routine. The correct sequence is of tremendous importance, and its logic must be understood and firmly entrenched in the rider's mind. If it is then conscientiously followed and practised from A to Z, the horse can be expected to progress steadily and without any serious difficulty towards his goal, mastering according to his natural ability each new step as he comes to it.

It is also intended, by dividing the whole thing into three-monthly periods, to give added stress to the idea of a logical sequence of major advances to be made, and at the same time, by thus introducing a series of obvious milestones, to encourage the rider to use these occasions for pause and reflection. Of course the choice of a specific number of months for each section is fairly arbitrary and must not be regarded as inflexible, but it does indicate the sort of time that the average horse is likely to require, and anything much less will be courting trouble and dis-appointment. Some may take longer and some even a shorter time, but three months should be sufficient for the horse to make useful progress in earlier work and at the same time to master a new lesson of major significance to the point where it will be safe to begin the next.

It has to be remembered that a horse possesses comparatively limited intelligence. This factor results in the energy and power being sometimes rather difficult to co-ordinate and control. This in turn means that it nearly always takes some time for a new lesson, however quickly picked up in the first place, to become assimilated into the horse's repertoire to the extent that it can be called into play at any moment without causing tension or over-excitement. The overall requirement for calmness in a good dressage or riding horse, no matter how difficult the task asked of him, thus becomes a controlling influence in regulating the speed of the training programme. The maintenance of calmness must be given priority over virtually all other considerations.

It will also be seen in the written programme that the schedule for each three-monthly period includes a call for recapitulation of the preceding exercises. This recapitulation is in practice a continuous and vital element in training and must never be forgotten or neglected. Each and all of the more advanced exercises depend directly for their successful performance on the degree of perfection attained in the imme-diately preceding work with a chain reaction working right back to the most basic lessons in obedience, suppleness, impulsion and so on. These basic matters must always be kept fresh and up to date, steadily improv-ing but never taken for granted.

Notes to outline programme

1. The considerations listed in each phase indicate the period in which that particular lesson or factor should be first introduced. They may be relisted in sub-sequent phases if they are of special or increasing importance.

2. **Bold** entries show the sequence and logical development of lessons in lateral work.

TWO-YEAR OUTLINE PROGRAMME

Phase	Months	Exercises and special considerations		
1	1–3	LUNGEING communication fitness balance confidence	obedience self-carriage suppleness	activity dexterity acceptance of the bit searching forward
2	4–6	RIDING calm contact forward straight	rhythm purity of paces searching forward **turn on** **forehand**	**half circle,** **qtrs out** forward leg response canter rein aids
3	7–9	recapitulation to the bit supple bends	transitions impulsion half-halts	canter **leg-yielding** trot to canter
4	10–12	recapitulation **shoulder-in** rein-back	walk to canter serpentines 15 m trot circles	canter changes through trot
5	13–15	recapitulation collection straightening more impulsion	**travers** medium trot more half-halts 10 m trot circles **turn on** **haunches**	15 m canter circles canter changes through walk 8 m trot half circles
6	16–18	recapitulation **trot half pass** simple changes	**renvers** medium canter 8 m trot circles	counter-canter lateral work on circles collected canter
7	19–21	recapitulation extended trot canter half pass	10 m canter circles more half-halts	inside leg responses canter to walk
8	22–24	recapitulation extended canter	flying changes double bridle	

PART II

Practical Work: The First Year

The author working Peter Jones on an economically designed lunge-ring.

CHAPTER SIX

Work on the Lunge
Phase 1 (Months 1–3)

Confidence. Communication. Obedience. Fitness. Self-carriage.
Activity. Suppleness. Dexterity. Acceptance of bit. Balance.
Searching forward. The paces.

Preparation

The day has arrived when, with all forethought and preparation behind us, we are to begin the work of training the young three- or four-year-old horse that has been on our premises long enough to feel thoroughly at home with his surroundings and with the personality of his trainer, the person who is to be his daily companion and guide for the next two years or more. We will have handled him, fed him, cleaned the stable, groomed him, picked out his feet and led him to and from the paddock or taken him grazing with a cavesson and long rein. In short, we will have established a happy relationship as a basis for everything that is to follow.

In addition to the cavesson he will be accustomed to wearing the lungeing roller both in and out of the stable and to having a snaffle bit in his mouth, though the latter should not be worn for long periods in the stable to prevent him developing the bad habit of playing with it with his tongue.

Our work over the whole three-month lungeing schedule that we hope to complete will be very greatly helped if we have been able to prepare the enclosed and all-weather ring mentioned in Part I, assuming of course that we do not have a covered school to work in. The ring will be particularly beneficial during the very first few days when there is little if any help from an assistant. We will assume that we have such a ring which is at least as good, and in some ways better, than the isolation of a covered school.

In this first lesson, it is best to put on his boots both in front and behind. It is possible, much later on when we know a good deal about his action and behaviour patterns, that we can dispense with boots on the hind legs, for convenience' sake. But they must never be left off the front legs, and it is wiser to retain them on the hind legs as well for all lungeing. That way we will not feel guilty of negligence if our horse should go lame behind.

It is a good thing to place the lungeing whip in the ring before leading the horse out of the stable. There will be enough on our hands at first without it, but in any case the lash should be twisted round the handle so as to avoid any risk of it getting tangled round our legs, or of causing any other inconvenience or alarm. We should certainly have created friendly acceptance of the whip as a normal part of life in the stable during the previous days, to the extent that the horse will allow himself to be touched on his neck and back with the handle, and if possible with the lash, without flinching.

Before leaving the stable, side reins should be attached to the middle or lower 'd's of the roller but not to the snaffle, the clip ends being also hooked on to the roller 'd's to keep them out of the way. They will not be needed for the first day or two.

Then, with the lunge-rein attached to the centre ring of the cavesson and with all the spare part carefully looped in the left hand, we lead the horse quietly to the ring. Having once again checked the gear and perhaps pulled up the girth-strap of the roller a hole or two, we pick up the whip in preparation for the first lesson.

The first day

Our sole purpose on this first day will be to get the horse used to his surroundings in general and to the lunge-ring and his gear in particular. We will ask for and expect nothing except that he should walk quietly round the ring-track on the left rein, that is to say, with the trainer on his near side.

If there is someone to help, he should lead the horse from the off side with a short leading rein also attached to the centre ring, while the trainer stands back about three metres, moving round parallel with the horse and in line with his shoulder. It would be unwise to stand in the centre of the ring because the full length of the lunge-rein, looping, perhaps scraping on the ground or billowing in the wind, might be upsetting and could be troublesome. But with only two or three metres of the rein let out it can be fully controlled, and there is no risk of it getting entangled in anybody's legs should the horse show any excitement and perhaps kick or plunge. In this way, he will be comforted and calmed by the close presence of the assistant while beginning to get the feel of his trainer being some little distance away on the end of a rein with little apparent direct control.

If there is no assistant we will have to lead the horse round the ring with a very shortened lunge-rein, just as when going to and from the stable. Frequently we stop and pat the horse and sometimes give him a nut or other tit-bit to make sure that he knows that we are pleased with him and that he has nothing whatever to fear. As with the assistant, we preface every action with a verbal signal or command, and acknowledge each obedient response with a further pat or with a grateful sounding voice. After two or three times round the ring in this way, and if all is going well, the reins can be eased out a little until we are out of direct contact with two or three metres of rein paid out. Great patience may be needed at this point to stop the horse turning in to come closer to us. At first we should just shorten the rein and lead him quietly back to the track and start again. But he may persist in which case we should try to maintain the required distance with an absolutely passive use of the whip pointed towards his shoulder. We may even need to give him a light prod with the butt, but on no account must force or fear be used to keep him away, only patience and perseverance. Do not expect too much this first day, and do not try to use too long a rein. The lesson should end after ten minutes or thereabouts, and if by that time we have succeeded in getting the pupil to walk twice round the track at the end of a three-metre rein, or even two metres, we can be well satisfied and will have made a good start. Halt him, still on the track, make much of him, and lead him back to the stable, with perhaps a few minutes' grazing on the way, and a bit of hay for him when he gets there.

First few days

The whole lesson for the first two days, or three if necessary, should be spent in this way, concentrating only on getting the horse to walk quietly round the track at a little distance from his trainer, accepting the idea of remote control, and halting when asked. This will all be done on the left rein only, until that lesson has been thoroughly absorbed. No attempt should be made to change over to the right rein until the left rein is firmly established, which is likely to be at least a week, until we can stand still in the centre of the ring with the horse remaining on the track. Only then should we begin the same lesson all over again, with the same detailed care, on the right rein. The fact that he has understood what is wanted of him on the left rein is no indication whatever that he will immediately 'catch on' when asked to do the same thing on the other rein, with his trainer in an altogether different position. He is likely to appear a little stupid and obstinate in his determination not to co-operate with the new game, but patience and firmness will soon put that right, and in less than two weeks in all he will be operating obediently in both directions.

Side reins

The side reins are not attached to the bit as yet, and there are two reasons for this. One is that there is quite enough for the horse to get used to and to assimilate on his first introduction to work without the worry of something attached directly to his mouth. And secondly, it is always inadvisable to use side reins for prolonged periods of walking, at which pace the horse requires great freedom of his head and neck, except very much later when he is able to perform a collected walk without becoming stiff and restricted in the back. But it is vitally important in the early stages of his education that he should develop a good swinging walk with the muscular movement flowing through an unrestricted back and neck and the hind legs stepping well past the prints of the forefeet.

The voice

We use the voice clearly and distinctly to initiate each and every action required of the horse, as well as to talk soothingly and encouragingly to him in exactly the same way as we have been used to doing in the stable. The vocal commands come from the trainer only, the assistant making no sound but reacting to the commands as if he were the horse. Apart from soothing or steadying noises, vocal signals will only be needed for walking forward and for halting on this first day, but signals will be added later for trotting, cantering, extending and perhaps several others. So right from the start we should adopt a tone and a pronunciation for walking and for halting that will sound altogether different from each other and from any signals that will be introduced later. Almost any signal will do as long as it is used with absolute consistency, but it is a good idea to use a lively tone of voice for a command requiring increased activity such as moving into a faster pace, and a gentle and lower tone when asking for reduced activity.

The trot

The trot should not be asked for, and indeed should be positively discouraged, during these first few days when the main object is to establish
a relationship based on calmness and confidence. A young horse tends
all too easily to get carried away, mentally as well as physically, by the
muscular exhilaration of trotting and disturbed, or even distressed, by the
sheer difficulty of keeping his balance at that pace on a continuous circle.
Often he will cease to pay any attention to the trainer and will trot round
at too fast a speed and as it were in a mental trance. It may be quite
impossible to stop the trot until the horse gets tired and falls back into a
walk in a state of bewildered exhaustion. That sort of happening is, of
course, the last thing we want especially when there is no understanding
of the command to halt, as it is the complete antithesis of the controlled and attentive co-operation that is the beginning and the end of
good training. To allow that kind of almost hysterical activity to develop
will also involve a considerable risk of physical injury or strain. If, nevertheless, we are overcome by circumstances and the horse breaks away
into a trot, our only course is to keep absolutely calm and to make
soothing noises for him to slow down into a walk of his own accord as
he finds the self-inflicted trot both tiring and boring.

There should be no fear of unwanted trotting so long as there is an
assistant. But once the walk on both reins has been satisfactorily settled,
there is no need for help. We will also then be ready to start work at the
trot, even if it is not offered by the horse. The slower the better should
be the motto for a day or two so that the horse can discover that the
command to trot is not an invitation to get a little excited.

Using side reins

Now it is time to clip the side reins to the bit as they will provide just
that little bit of control and will tend to give the horse something to
think about besides exploiting the semi-freedom that he feels at the end
of the lunge. Try them out for length first at the walk, and be satisfied
if they are short enough to exert a very small amount of control and
influence on the angle of the face at that pace. Then when you ask for a
trot they will appear to have virtually no influence at all unless he throws
his head about in a disobedient or over-playful manner or pokes his
nose. And that is how they should be for a day or two, until he has got
thoroughly used to them. But even then we must remember that

at this stage the main purpose of the side reins is to place and keep the bit in such a position that the horse will be encouraged to reach forward to make and maintain contact with it. They must never be shortened so that the bit is brought back to a position where the horse is unable to avoid contact with it. The contact must be of his own choosing, and he will have to make a positive physical effort to achieve it. It is the job of the trainer not to make it impossible for him to do this by having the side reins too long, and yet to ensure that he does make the required effort. Only thus can we make a beginning at the long process of stretching the horse's spine and thereby freeing the back muscles so that they can be made supple, strong and active.

Forward boldness

It is worth repeating that the first lessons are aimed at teaching the horse to walk boldly forward without fear or inhibition, and that boldness must not be impeded by tight side reins that restrict the movement. Once the initial calmness and confidence has been won, the horse, with or without the assistant to lead him, must never be allowed to hang back so that the trainer appears to be pulling him along with the lunge-rein. The trainer must always endeavour to stand opposite the horse's shoulder so that the horse appears to take the lead, and will feel that he is doing so. Psychologically, this is fundamental to the whole training process and to the gradual development of impulsion which is the mainspring to all successful equestrian activity.

For the first week or ten days we are concerned solely with obtaining calmness, confidence and obedience. The horse should be thoroughly relaxed and consequently receptive. But that is only a means to an end, and we then start to make use of that receptiveness by asking for a little more activity in the work, for a more positive approach that will begin to make some real demands on the physique of the horse. But the extra activity must be brought out of the initially relaxed pupil only because the trainer has asked for it. It will be of little value if it emanates from over-excitement combined with general inattentiveness on the part of the horse, or if he is using his excessive activity merely to evade the serious purpose of the lesson. So for this reason it is essential to maintain the ability to revert to relaxation at will so that you can be sure that the work is genuine and can be properly controlled. Periods of real and steadily increasing activity are interspersed with frequent short periods of relaxation. This may be easier said than done, but the trainer should continue to strive for this degree of control right through the schedule and should always beware of confusing excitement with genuine and purposeful activity which alone will produce the type of fitness and physical development that we hope to bring about.

Reaching down

During the relaxed periods we want to encourage and induce the horse to lower his head and neck, to reach forwards and downwards to the extent that his muzzle may be only a foot or less from the ground. This is a very beneficial exercise in that it stretches and frees all the muscles of the back and neck and relaxes the poll. This is achieved partly as a result of the horse becoming bored and consequently relaxed, and partly by the indication of the trainer's lowered rein hand. It is an exercise that the trainer will be well advised to resort to periodically throughout all his work as a means of ensuring that the back is not becoming permanently taut. There is always a great danger that the muscles of the back, shoulders and neck will not stay supple partly because the mere weight of the rider tends to depress and suppress them, and partly as a result of the determination of over-ambitious riders to maintain a high head carriage before the back has become strong enough to carry the forehand lightly in front of slightly lowered quarters. So from the start we must be aware of this danger and must frequently check, by exercises such as the one just mentioned, that all is well.

The need to practise this exercise provides another good reason why the side reins must not be fitted at all short at this early stage. Later, when they will often be worn considerably shorter, they can be unfastened for certain periods. Care should be taken, when the horse is moving in this way, to maintain the freedom and length of the stride.

The whip

These early lessons in walk or slow trot provide a good opportunity to accustom the horse to being touched with the lash as well as the shaft of the lunge-whip. The lash can be lightly laid across his back or quarters and then allowed to slide quietly off as he moves forward. This can be repeated many times until it comes to be regarded almost as a caress or a mild sedative.

The whip is brought into play very gradually, but it soon becomes an essential part of lungeing. Once the grammar of communication has been learnt, the whip will be in almost constant play for one purpose or another. The two chief aspects of its work are to keep the horse out at the full length of the rein so that there is a light contact without being taut, and as a means of sustaining or increasing activity and impulsion from the quarters. Both these effects can be achieved either by swinging the lash with a long smooth movement from rear to front without actually touching the horse, or by throwing the end of the lash, lightly but accurately as a fisherman throws a fly with his rod, so that it just touches a chosen spot on the horse which may be his shoulder, signifying keep out, or his quarters, or his hind legs above the hocks, signifying more activity. The keep-out message can also be passed just by pointing the tip of the whip shaft at his forehand, without using the lash at all. In any case it is of great importance, as has been pointed out in Part I of this book, that the overall length of the whip should be long enough to permit the trainer to touch the horse at any time while the latter is on the track and the former pivoting firmly on his heel on the centre point of the ring. If the whip is any shorter it will without question have a seriously adverse effect on the results achieved on the lunge, due to the fact that the whip either becomes an empty threat or else the trainer is constantly getting off balance through moving closer to the horse in order to reach him. It is also important that the trainer should always remain pivoting on his centre spot so that the horse can learn to move and work on a perfect circle while retaining a steady contact with the lunge-rein. If the trainer moves, the horse will inevitably increase or decrease the diameter of his circle and will find it very difficult to establish a steady rhythm.

Bending and suppleness

It is the steady rhythm of stride, performed on an absolutely regular circle, that, with practice, makes the horse bend himself to conform to the curve of the circle on which he is working. This is the beginning of lateral suppleness. But each time a movement by the trainer allows the horse to fall out from the true circle, the horse will straighten himself and so temporarily lose the bending and suppling effect. His balance will be interfered with and he will be inclined to shorten rather than lengthen his stride.

Besides its suppling effect, trotting on a circle is also an exercise in dexterity and co-ordination for the horse. The outside pair of legs have to move on a bigger circle than the inner pair, and consequently the outer ones have to take slightly longer steps in order to keep up with the inner pair. But this adjustment is further complicated for the horse by the fact that he trots on alternate diagonals. It follows that the inner leg of each diagonal, which will be the foreleg in one case and the hind leg in the other, will have to shorten its length of step while its outer half of the diagonal will be lengthening. It is small wonder that perfect balance and rhythm on small circles are quite difficult to achieve. It is a lesson in eurhythmics and consequently of dexterity.

Dexterity

Dexterity also improves every time the trainer asks for a transition from one pace to another on the circle. From walk to trot and vice versa, and later from walk or trot into canter and vice versa, the co-ordination and adjustment by the horse of his leg actions have perforce to be slightly but significantly modified as compared with the same movement carried out on a straight line. A two-legged animal such as man has no similar experience, its mechanical processes being far simpler, so the trainer must make due allowances for a certain amount of initial clumsiness and fumbling by his horse.

We also have to consider more than the ability to work in correct rhythm on a circle: we have to develop and confirm the ability to act equally easily on either rein. This problem arises, however slightly, with all horses because of their innate tendency to be less than straight in their spine. They find it easier to bend to one side than to the other, the difficulty being noticeable in the muscles of the neck as well as in the body. This natural phenomenon, which may never be entirely over-come, has to be worked on throughout the horse's education with patience and persistence to minimize its effect on the symmetry of the horse's paces and his response to the aids. In lunge work, the only remedial actions open to the trainer are to do rather more work on the difficult rein (the stiff side) than on the easy one, and to ensure that the horse is not allowed to lean on the cavesson and hang towards the outside of the ring. By using the latter trick, which is really a form of evasion, the horse is able to maintain the easy concave bend on his outer side, with the result that the work on that particular rein does nothing to supple the stiff muscles on the inner side. He has to be prevented from leaning out by repeated and persistent tugs at the lunge-rein inter-spersed with short moments of relative freedom in which he is encou-raged to carry himself without the contact of the lunge-rein. This may not show immediate results, but it will succeed with patience, if only because in time the horse will grow tired of the corrective tugs and will try to find a manner of going that will avoid them. Then, as soon as he gets the message and begins to work in free balance, he will automatically begin to adjust himself to the curve of the lunge-ring, even when working on the different rein with the stiff side towards the trainer. It will even then take time and some skill to make that side supple, but that is a problem that every trainer has to overcome.

Then also under the heading of dexterity comes the ability to change gait as well as speed neatly, accurately and promptly, without loss of balance or rhythm. This has to be learned, over a long period, by means of frequent and repeated transitions of all sorts, combined with a determination by the trainer to be a strict perfectionist. Sloppiness, provided the horse has not been asked to do something too difficult for his state of training, is always equivalent to evasiveness, which in turn may be due to idleness. The trainer's response to a sloppy reaction from his pupil should be first to check that the question was fair and that he has asked it in a reasonable and intelligible way at a reasonable moment, and then to repeat the challenge calmly, firmly and clearly, determined that he will get a better answer the second time. A touch with the whip at the right moment and on the right spot will often produce a wonderful improvement in the speed and the energy of the horse's responses: just the lightest touch with the tip of the lash above the hock for more drive from behind, or perhaps in the area of the girth or by the elbow to ask for more movement in front.

Shortening the side reins

As the horse gradually improves in his balance and thereby in his ability to respond quickly and easily to the trainer's demands to improve or change the pace, we begin with great caution to shorten the side reins a little bit at a time and probably not more often than about two holes a week. As he learns to work without the bit being in any way an interference, so we can begin to make greater demands on his physical efforts. We do this by shortening, by means of the side reins, the length of the frame in which we want the horse to work. At this stage the side reins should be at such a length that the line of the horse's face, when he is trotting calmly forward, will be about ten degrees in front of the vertical, though we shall also aim, nearer the end of the three months' lunge period, to be able to work the horse in the more collected position of about five degrees, but never less than that except for very short periods.

A vertical position of the face should never be attempted on a young horse in side reins for several very good reasons. First, the horse will not have got anywhere near the state of muscular strength, elasticity and self-control that is necessary for him to hold that position voluntarily. And secondly, whereas the rider of an advanced horse can instantaneously release the rein restriction when he senses that he has asked enough, or when the movement requiring that position has been completed, the lunge trainer has no means of quick adjustment of the side reins when he senses or sees that the horse needs the reward of release – nor will his eyes tell him as quickly as the feel from the saddle. The horse has to be halted before any such adjustment can be made. Not only does such a process take quite a long time, but it also must be remembered that any given length of side rein is always much more restrictive at the walk or the halt than it is in the trot. So the horse has to suffer increased restriction before he can be released. Obviously, this is a psychologically and physically harmful process which must not be practised.

The reason why a horse can accept and adapt himself to rather shorter side reins in the trot than in walk or at the halt lies in the mechanical fact that the trot is a simple two-beat pace of perfect symmetry with a moment of suspension between each beat. That moment of suspension is sufficient to allow the natural flexibility of the spine including the neck to come into play thereby slightly reducing the overall length. In the walk, and of course at the halt, there is no total suspension between any of the footfalls and consequently the spine, between the withers and the croup, is always at its full length. Any restriction imposed at those paces by the side reins necessarily acts solely on the neck which is undesirable as well as being uncomfortable for the horse.

Provided the side reins are shortened little by little in accord with the gradual development of the horse, both mental and physical, they will have the purely beneficial effect of encouraging the horse to adopt and work in a more positive and upright form of self-carriage. He will always try not to pull or to lie on the bit, and in order to avoid doing that he will inevitably find himself having to work harder with the muscles of his quarters and back. In short, he will try to balance himself by the greater engagement of his quarters as the only alternative to leaning on the bit. And therein lies the essence of the whole art of dressage, and we shall have begun to flavour it, with the help of side reins, before we ever climb on our horse's back. We must, however always be on the watch to ensure that the side reins are not shortened to the point where they impede the freedom of the shoulders and the length of the stride.

Self-carriage

To a very large extent, self-carriage and acceptance of the bit go hand in hand and are complementary. By acceptance of the bit we mean the willingness of the horse calmly to accept whatever directions and restraints the rider may impose on him by means of the reins. It is misleading to suggest, as is sometimes done, that accepting the bit and being 'on the bit' are one and the same thing. It is quite possible for a horse to be accepting the bit, in the literal sense, while being technically above it, or even behind it. Being on the bit requires the head to be approaching the vertical, as described previously, so that it is geometrically and mechanically possible for the muscular thrust from the quarters to pass through the back and neck to the mouth and so back to the rider's hands and through them to his seat. If the head is too far in front of the vertical, beginning in extreme cases to approach the horizontal, the thrust will be blocked at the withers by the rein tension coming back from the mouth through the poll and neck instead of direct to the hand. It is as well that the trainer should keep the distinction between these two aspects of the horse's education very clear in his mind. He should have no difficulty in having his horse used to and in the habit of working 'on the bit', as well as accepting it, well before the time comes to begin mounted work.

The paces

The trainer must remember that, in this period of work on the lunge, he is laying the foundation and the seeds of everything that is to follow. The quality of any horse's work, and the pleasure to be obtained from it, relies more than anything else upon the purity of the paces: that is, the freedom, the power and the rhythm of each and every step. It must, therefore, be the trainer's prime object in each and every lesson on the lunge further to improve the simple or basic paces. To do this he must strive to check any tendency to hurry the tempo by using his voice to calm and by little checks with the lunge-rein. But he must also use his whip, and perhaps his voice, to create and to maintain a degree of energy in the regular thrust of the hind legs that will, through the slight increase in suspension created by the energy, tend to lengthen the amount of ground covered by each stride. Thus freedom of movement is created, the freedom that is visibly expressed by the swing of the shoulders and the desire of the horse to lengthen his neck, both aspects caused by the uninhibited flow of energetic muscular action from the quarters through the back and into the forehand.

The difficulty, of course, is to prevent the lengthening of the step leading to a hurried or running tempo, and herein lies the skill of the trainer and the counterplay between the controlling action of the rein and the activating influence of the whip, the latter being used mainly in long, slow sweeps past the horse from rear to front alternated occasionally with light but precise touches on the body or limbs. Gradually, as the hind legs learn to be more and more active in relation to the speed at which the horse is moving, so they will come to the ground just that little bit further under the horse, thus taking more weight off the forehand and freeing the shoulders and forelegs. The results aimed at in this context are not easily or quickly achieved, but a very little of what is wanted makes a very big difference to the bearing of the horse, to his agility, and consequently to his ability to master the more complicated or demanding exercises that will be required of him later on.

The canter

The canter is a pace that tends to have special problems concerning balance and calmness which require great patience to overcome. A young horse can canter on a straight line probably as easily as he can trot, but it is a much more complicated affair for him to do so on a relatively small circle. The simple symmetry of the trot sequence can be fairly easily adapted to the curved line, whereas the canter is unsymmetrical and at times totally on the forehand, i.e. when the whole weight of the horse is supported on the leading foreleg. The canter can also be irregular, the lead can be changed, it is all too frequently crooked, and it can engender excitement and consequent inattention.

Not every horse experiences difficulties, but where they do exist, they must be given special consideration, with appropriate adjustments to the programme. Any difficulties in the canter will be much more acute on the lunge than they would be when mounted.

It is best not to try to introduce the canter until the horse has acquired an established balance in trot as well as a degree of mental equilibrium, or calm confidence in his trainer. When these factors are assured it will be time enough to try the canter, because he will then be better able to grapple with such problems that do arise without falling around or developing an anxiety complex about the pace. Of course, if the horse offers the canter and is clearly confident and comfortable in that pace, then there is no need to be worried about it, though it will still be advisable to restrict its use to a minimum for at least the first month. It will be all the better when the time is ripe. If there are obvious difficulties, it may be unwise to insist on the canter for up to two months, and in extreme cases it can be best to exclude it altogether from the lunge programme and wait till it can be slipped in when mounted work is progressing satisfactorily on straight lines in the open.

With some horses it may be difficult to obtain a canter at all to begin with. Efforts to produce one may end only in the trot becoming faster and faster, not to say hysterical and uncontrollable. Such a situation is not uncommon and must be treated with great patience and tact to avoid the horse building up a mental complex about the very idea of the canter. The trainer should never resort to using the whip in a threatening or frightening manner to obtain a canter. Better to wait until one day it will happen quite easily, perhaps even by chance.

If the horse does offer a canter of his own accord, it can be accepted and appreciated by the voice, telling him it is a *canter . . . canter . . . canter* so that he will associate the pace with the command.

The first time the horse canters, he can be allowed to continue for a maximum of one or two complete circles. If he has not reverted to the trot or walk by that time, every effort should be made by the use of the voice and by gentle tugging on the lunge-rein to slow down the canter and obtain the trot. The thing to avoid at all costs is the impression that the canter means an opportunity for a good lark and is a means of taking control away from the trainer. So because it tends to be exciting, and because it is tiring, it should be practised only for very short spells followed by a calming walk or steady trot and, very frequently, by a reward.

It often helps to induce the canter from the trot if the horse is first drawn by the lunge-rein into a slightly smaller circle and then, at the moment the command to canter is given, allowed to slip back into the larger circle again and thus experience a feeling of increased freedom.

It will not be necessary to alter the length of the side reins for the canter because, on the whole, it naturally tends to produce a more elevated outline than the natural trot, and the more pronounced period of suspension, after the third beat of the pace, gives the horse room to adapt himself to whatever frame is set for him by the reins.

Backing

During the last week or two of the three months' lungeing period, the horse can be backed in the normal quiet and careful way. It is best to obtain some assistance for this process if that is at all possible. In that case it can be done in the lungeing ring, and the horse then led round by the assistant (or the trainer) on a short rein until he appears to have accepted the novelty.

It is a good thing to spend a short time at the end of the next few days of lungeing in going through all the main sections and transitions of the work that he has already learned, but with the rider on this back. This mounted work inside the ring should be quite brief and not too much activity should be demanded, because of the unbalancing effect that the weight of the rider will exert. That added problem will be accentuated by any shortcoming in the rider's ability to follow the unbalanced movement of the young horse. It will, therefore, be wise to plan to move out of the ring into more open places for daily work just as soon as a reasonable degree of mutual confidence has been established.

Cavaletti

Quite a lot of cavaletti work and jumping can be carried out on the lunge, beginning of course with ground bars. It will help to keep the horse fresh and keen and interested, as well as being a first-class exercise for improving the action and flexibility of the joints, and for stretching the back muscles. It will also greatly increase his suppleness and dexterity.

Main aspects of lungeing

So we work steadily on, trying to add a little improvement each day but more likely taking a week to achieve significant changes. If we try to take a comprehensive view of the lunge work, we should see it as broken down into four predominant sections. They are:

1. *Preparation for riding*, covering physical fitness and self-carriage.
2. *Regularity and rhythm of the paces*, born of calm, repetitive and active work.
3. *Suppleness*, both lateral and longitudinal, but primarily the former, born of consistent work on the circle.
4. *Attention, obedience and confidence*, born of the fearless acceptance of the powerful control exercised by the cavesson, the lunge-rein and the whip.

A fine Thoroughbred working well in the early stages. Mrs R. N. Hall on Abound.

CHAPTER SEVEN

Early Riding
Phase 2 (Months 4–6)

Calm. Straight lines. Forward movement. Contact. Rhythm.
Purity of pace. Searching forward. Forward leg response.
Turn on the forehand. Half circle, quarters out. Canter.

Preliminary work

The horse has now been backed and accustomed to accepting that experience without alarm or mental disturbance. He has been ridden round the lunge-ring for a few minutes at the end of the lunge lesson for the last four or five days and has also been led, mounted of course, round the more open spaces of the stable yard and his own well-known paddock. All this has been done very quietly, with just a little trotting at a very slow speed inside the ring to introduce him to the feel of the rider's weight at that pace.

So we can ride our young horse, but it is unwise and unreasonable to discard the lunge-ring altogether. We must remember that the rider's weight is considerable and that the additional strain on the horse's muscles will be sudden and severe. It is a big jump from carrying nothing to carrying eleven or twelve stone, and we want to avoid anything that will cause the horse to associate being ridden with any form of stress, strain or ache. It is therefore best to combine lungeing and riding in the daily programme for at least the first ten days of this phase. Lunge for fifteen to twenty minutes and then ride for the same length of time. That way there will be no sudden change in the routine; any surplus steam will be let off on the lunge, and we shall avoid tiring those vital muscles in the horse's back.

For the same first ten days the ridden work should be mainly in walk on a long rein, interspersed with very short periods of quiet rising trot. If possible this should be done in a not too big field or paddock where there is the minimum likelihood of sudden disturbance, the whole purpose and object being to accustom the horse to working without the control of the lunge-rein and cavesson and to being guided by the rider through the reins and the snaffle. In doing this, the rider must constantly remind himself that up to now the snaffle bit has been a purely passive thing that has exerted no direct influence of any kind on the horse's mouth. He has got used to it and is not afraid of it. He has learned to work with it on his own terms, but it has never made any demands on him. It is perfectly natural, therefore, that he will fail to respond sensibly to the initial requests by the rider, passed to him through the reins and bit, that he should halt or turn right or left, or even just slow down. This new form of language has to be introduced very carefully and tactfully, over a period of many days, by combining the new signals with the old and well-understood voice messages to which he has learned to respond so accurately on the lunge. Neglect of this problem must result in some degree of misunderstanding and consequent mental or physical pain to the horse, more particularly to the sensitive and important bars of the mouth.

There have been no vocal signals for turning right or left, and that is one of the reasons why all the very early ridden work should be restricted. as far as possible to straight lines. All changes of direction should be made gently and progressively, the rein aid being given in a broadly 'opening' manner with great care not to give the horse the impression that he is being forced. This lesson, like so many others, should be taught and established at the walk before trying it out in trot because in walk the horse is far less likely to lose his balance and so to find himself physically unable to respond freely and without resistance.

Once a reasonable degree of mutual confidence has been established and the rider is fairly sure that the horse will not try to dislodge him, use can be made of quiet lanes or tracks as an alternative to the home paddock or field. The walk should be the primary pace with a long but not loose rein. A light contact should be kept, not least because it maintains the conversation between the two parties and reduces the chance of the rider being caught unawares by a sudden shy or jump. There will also be less tendency for the rider to grab the reins in a violent manner as might happen if they had been hanging loose in the first instance.

Whether in the paddock or on tracks, the rider should endeavour to maintain a lively and active pace in walk as well as in trot. Begin as you intend to go on, and try to create a habit of a good walk though without too regular or excessive leg aids. The trot should be used for very short stretches at first, perhaps fifty to a hundred yards at a time and then back to a walk, and always a rising trot so as to put the minimum strain on the undeveloped back muscles. This frequent trot–walk sequence will greatly help to keep the horse calm which is of vital importance at all times but never more so than now. Every time a change of pace is called for the voice should be used first, followed closely by the appropriate leg and rein aid, until the latter are understood and the former can be discontinued.

Since the calm acceptance by the horse of the human partnership in his future life and work will play a major part in the successful outcome of his training, it will be wise to try to plan things so as positively to avoid the risk of alarm or disturbance. Introduce him to light and slow traffic before you ask him to face lorries. Don't ride too close to a hedgerow on a windy day when the branches are waving about. Try to think well ahead to keep out of unnecessary trouble which might result in your having a tussle with the horse just to keep him in reasonable control.

After about a fortnight of these preliminary aspects of ridden work, we can begin to phase out the lungeing and concentrate on the daily routine under saddle. Once again let us remember that the lunge is a wonderful refresher, both psychologically and physically, and it can do nothing but good to continue to use it as the main and only lesson on one day in each week. It will refresh the trainer as well as the horse, if only from the pleasure he will get from watching the steady development of his pupil. And of course it will also equip him with accumulating knowledge about the horse on which he can base his ridden programme. Sight is always more perceptive than feel and consequently regular lunge periods are particularly valuable to those who do all or most of their training without the help or supervision of someone on the ground.

Forward movement

The prevailing factor to be kept in mind throughout the whole of this first three months under the saddle, and indeed in all phases of training, is the need to encourage and maintain free forward movement. Without it, nothing good can be done, and since we start with nothing we must make free forward movement our very first requirement, to be established to the extent that it becomes second nature to the horse and can be obtained by the rider, without question, on demand.

This is so vitally important that it is worth checking that we really know quite clearly what we mean by the phrase. To begin with, forward movement is in the very nature of any horse. He does not move sideways or backwards with great ease and in general will only do so by himself to avoid something. Later on in the training we shall need to work on both those aspects of motion in order to develop full control and as gymnastic exercises, but it would be a serious mistake to introduce them in any form at this early stage as they can all too easily be used by the horse as an evasion of the energetic physical requirements of going forward.

Willingness

Forward movement in itself will need no explanation, but the word 'free' justifies a moment's thought. It is used here in two ways, both of them important. The movement, in whatever pace, must first of all be free in the sense that it is given to the rider without reservation immediately it is called for by the aids. It is the forward urge felt by and received into the rider's hands.

This may sound obvious, and even easy, but that is not always the case with every horse. The unwanted reservations can exist or creep in from many sources and much tact and determination may have to be employed to overcome and eradicate them.

The horse may be a little unco-operative with the result that the rider may quite clearly feel him say 'I won't', just for an instant or even longer, when the aid has signalled forward. He may be physically lazy or lethargic so that he seems to ignore the forward request until it has to be repeated a second time. Another cause for unwillingness to go forward with real freedom might be the weakness or stiffness of certain muscles, though this would be less likely, unless the horse is over-tired, than either of the former examples. But whatever the cause of the undesirable holding back, it must never be overlooked or neglected. As the days and weeks go by we must become more and more strict and demanding in our efforts to create the habit of willing obedience to our requests. We can, and indeed must, make concessions for youth and immaturity as regards the manner in which the horse is able to comply, but we should make fewer and fewer concessions as regards the immediacy of the response.

Basically, it is the response to the leg aid that we want more than anything else. If we allow the young horse to think that he can disregard those aids with impunity, he will very soon settle into the habit of slovenly and even disrespectful behaviour out of which it will be difficult to progress. The discipline of the aids has to be accepted from the beginning. There is no need to be unkind or violent; if the leg is ignored, don't go on kicking, but rather supplement it with a tap from the whip. If the whip taps are ignored, don't go on tapping, but touch him with the spur.

We work as much as possible on long straight lines, gradually requiring and acquiring a light but absolutely constant, steady and equal contact with the mouth with both reins. It is very important that the rider's hands should be held in the correct manner and at the correct height: i.e. with straight wrists, thumbs uppermost and in an exactly straight line between the elbow and the bit. This is the position in which they can and will be most sensitive to the horse's needs and most able to follow and encourage the forward flow of the movement through the horse, but without breaking or altering the contact. The rider should constantly be asking himself whether his hands and arms and shoulders are relaxed, sensitive, communicative and generous. These points need constant checking with even the most experienced riders, in order to ensure that the young horse is in no way inhibited in his free forward movement.

Laziness is perhaps the most difficult of the three aspects of reluctance to deal with. Something less than a reprimand but more than mere sympathy may then be needed to produce the activity that is essential for any progressive training. The whip may have to be called into play to reinforce the legs sooner than would otherwise be expected and even spurs may be required, though their introduction should be postponed on principle for at least a month or so, and even then they should be used only after very careful thought and study of the horse's psychology and as a last resort. Spurs can all too easily be resented by young horses, and the resentment can easily become a habit, so they should in any case be used only by riders who are sufficiently knowledgeable and skilful to use them correctly and, even more important, to be able to refrain from using them.

Unconstrained movement

The second sense in which forward movement must be free is purely physical and concerns the loose and unconstrained way in which the horse uses its muscles and limbs. He has to be taught and encouraged to make full use of the joints and muscles of his whole body, to develop and use his full power. Some horses will be able to do this better than others, quite naturally, but all can and need to be improved in this respect by exercises carried on throughout their training. A few daily exercises in the bedroom or in the gymnasium will work wonders in loosening and suppling a human body, and the same thing applies to the horse in the development of his athleticism. Without this looseness and freedom of limb we shall not be able to achieve the type of free forward movement that we need. Gentleness, tact and sympathy must be employed together with a temporary reduction in the frequency with which the physical effort is demanded, until the horse is strong enough to give free forward movement.

We concentrate, therefore, in our early ridden work on teaching the horse to accept, to the extent that he comes to act almost instinctively, that he must at all times be pushing forward with enthusiasm and diligence. It is not sufficient to be just moving calmly in the required direction in a quiet but not particularly enthusiastic manner. There must be an urge and a drive that indicates generosity and may even have to be restrained a little. Not every young horse begins by acting in quite this generous way, but a great deal can be done to establish a habit, an attitude to life, that is an improvement on what the horse could offer in the first place.

Rhythm

Next in importance to the freedom and spontaneity of forward movement, the rider must concern himself with the establishment of an absolutely steady and regular rhythm in each of the three paces. This must become second nature to the horse and can only be achieved by calmness and quiet acceptance of the bit, which results in a steady and consistent carriage, combined with balance and just sufficient impulsion for the current stage of work. With so many essential ingredients it is clearly not an altogether easy job, and we had better take a look at each element in turn.

Before doing so we should be absolutely clear in our minds about the true meaning of rhythm. Some misunderstanding can occur if the word is used in a loose or ill-defined manner. The word and its conception occur in very many different spheres of life, some abstract and some concrete, and there is no all-embracing definition and none that has universal acceptance for equitation. Nevertheless, it is not so difficult as all that and we shall not go far wrong if we accept that rhythm is 'the regularity and correctly ordered flow of the pace'. That means, with just a little elaboration, that each step and stride must, in increasing order of difficulty:

(a) accurately maintain the correct order or sequence of footfall, four beats for walk, two beats for trot and three beats for canter;
(b) maintain a smooth flow from each step or stride to the next;
(c) maintain a perfect regularity of beat as if it were controlled by a metronome.

If these three aspects of our chosen definition of rhythm can be achieved and held, then the horse, the rider and the spectator will experience a sensation of thrill and satisfaction. There is no doubt that horses respond well to music when they are working, and they will by the same token respond to the rhythm that they themselves generate with the aid of their rider.

In trying to develop this feeling of rhythm in a young horse the rider will need to ensure that he is not asking or even allowing the horse to go faster than the speed at which he can comfortably maintain his own balance. If the rider pushes the horse beyond that speed there will be a tendency for the steps to get shorter and faster, like the steps of a small child who finds himself losing his balance while running down a steep hill. The rider should therefore constantly try to find a compromise between steadying the pace but maintaining forward impulsion up to the bit.

It is not necessary to get involved in the question of impulsion at this stage, even though we have begun to mention it in our discussions. We shall discuss it in detail in the next chapter because by that time, after three months' steady forward riding, it will become a factor of major importance. But for this first three months it is sufficient to concentrate only on teaching our horse to work with a steady acceptance of and contact with the bit. This is done by gently but firmly urging the horse forward with the leg aids and at the same time gently and quietly taking the required contact – very light at first – with the reins which must be held with extremely sensitive and sympathetic hands. Once the contact is taken the hands must endeavour to follow every movement of the horse's head and, in particular, those movements which he makes in an effort to evade the contact. Often he will try to drop the contact by withdrawing his head, opening his mouth or shortening his neck. But whatever form the evasion takes, the hands must follow so as to maintain the contact with the least possible variation. In that way the horse will learn that he cannot evade the issue, that there is no point in trying to; and that there is nothing unpleasant about it, anyway. In fact he will come to find that a steady contact is helpful and gives him confidence in his movements. Which of course is exactly what we want. As the horse begins to move with that increasing confidence and rhythm, so the rider begins to feel an increasing awareness of, and ultimately a sense of controlling, each and every stride. So the long-term vision begins to open up, and the essence of it all is the early establishment of this steady, constant, comfortable contact with the reins. It may take a little time for the horse to accept this idea, so tact, sympathy and perseverance are needed.

If the rider gets the feeling that the contact is dwindling, he should, by the use of increased leg aids, insist that it is the horse that retakes the desired degree of contact by moving forward with more energy and determination, rather than the rider recovering it by pulling back with his hands. At the same time as he urges the horse forward he must not allow any increase in the actual speed by an easing of the hands. If he allows that to happen the horse will in effect be chasing a contact that is constantly evading him and he will get discouraged and lose his rhythm. But there is a world of difference between an action of the hands that restrains or forbids an increase in pace and one that pulls back in order to regain a lost contact. The latter must always be avoided as it transgresses the golden rule that all transitions or adjustments of pace should be performed primarily from behind with an increased engagement of the quarters. That concept will be discussed in the next chapter.

Methods of communication

It is of prime importance during this early riding period to establish the language that will enable the rider to communicate with his horse, without the use of the voice, on a wide variety of subtle matters. The voice was both essential and sufficient while the educational process was confined to lunge work, but it immediately becomes obvious when riding starts that the voice is much too clumsy and too limited a tool for the infinite variety of messages that we wish to be able to send in a flash to our mount. Between human beings the voice can do marvellous things, but only if there is time to make full use of all its possible nuances. If its use is confined to one short shout or whisper, meanings become limited.

Fortunately, we have all the facilities for quick and subtly varied conversation at our disposal, provided we learn to make full use of the potential range and scope of our arms, hands, legs, seat and weight. Let no rider think that this is a simple skill. It would not be easy to become proficient in the degree of bodily control required to convey the messages we have in mind even if we were sitting on a stationary wooden horse. We also have to learn to be skilful and subtle when sitting on and controlling an uneducated animal whose own movements are comparatively unpredictable and who requires help in the co-ordination of his own limbs. This is just another instance of the importance of the rider taking very seriously his own qualifications for undertaking the education of a horse. These qualifications are by no means impossible or even exceptionally difficult to acquire, but they do require some study and some practice, much of which, like the matter of suppleness already discussed, can be done on the ground and indoors.

For the moment we can reduce the problems to its three main ingredients: the body, the hands and the legs. During this phase of our work, the body is mainly concerned with not interfering with the young horse's efforts to discover his own balance under the rider. The hands are concerned mainly with encouraging and maintaining a steady, regular contact with the mouth, through relaxed and sensitive wrists and elbows. The use of the legs is a little more complicated, and it is necessary to discuss their use in some detail.

Leg aids

The use of the rider's legs in all equitation, shared to a greater or lesser extent with the influence of the seat, is to create and to control activity, and above all else to create forward movement. As the young horse's vocabulary is developed, we shall find that there is a very wide variety of types of activity to be called for or controlled, in fact, as many as there are degrees of collection and speed. It is obviously going to be essential that the horse should, without hesitation or misunderstanding, be able to interpret the particular type of activity being called for at any given moment. It would be most unreasonable to expect this of him unless we are able to use a different leg aid, or combination of leg and seat aids, for each and every type of action, or at least the several main types of action, that we are likely to require. It is therefore totally insufficient just to use our legs indiscriminately, perhaps more or less powerfully, in the same manner regardless of exactly what we are trying to say. We have to establish, and then use with total consistency, a leg alphabet. If we make it simple and logical we shall have no difficulty in obtaining response and co-operation from the horse.

We will deal first with the neutral or no-action position of the rider's legs. This is simple in that they should be lightly and always touching the horse from the seat bone downwards, with the lower part of the calf just immediately behind the girth. That is the most sensitive part of the horse's rib-cage; it is the most natural position for the legs, and it is the position from which the horse will most readily feel the smallest movement or variation of the leg, indicating that something new is being asked. To move the legs when nothing is asked is merely muddling and should never occur even if the rider is sitting talking to a friend. We sit on our horse only a short time each day, and we should not waste any of those precious moments by allowing ourselves to adopt sloppy habits which are bound to result in sloppy, vague reactions from our pupil.

Leg aids must be as gentle as possible, consistent with the ability of the horse to respond, and should be applied tactfully and progressively. That is to say, they should not be abrupt. Every rider will know that the horse's transitions should be prompt but smooth rather than abrupt, but we sometimes forget that this will only be achieved if our aids also have a degree of discretion.

The most frequently used aid or signal is the one to go forward, or to go forward more energetically. Ideally, all leg aids should be light and not call for any exaggerated or tiring effort from the rider. The precise meaning we wish to convey should therefore be clear without having to rely on different degrees of strength or pressure. An increased inward pressure from the normal or neutral position of the leg may be required as a call to attention or as a warning that a definite message is on the way. Consequently, if the message is to be a call for prompt forward, or increased forward, action, it will help if it is something other than a straight inward pressure. The most common, not to say universal, method of calling on forward action is the age-old backward kick. It may be a violent kick with a spur, or it may be a relatively gentle backward movement of the leg against the ribs and away from the girth. The latter may not be cruel, but it is just as illogical as the former. No doubt both methods can be made to produce forward action from the horse, but only because in principle they make the horse, or threaten to make the horse, too uncomfortable to stay where he is. He will go forward in order to get out of discomfort. If we want the intelligent co-operation of our horse we must clearly use a more intelligent form of communication than that. We express our wish to go forward by a distinct inward and forward action of the leg. In practice, the forward element of the action is barely visible to an onlooker though it is just sufficient to rub against the lie of the hair and will be clearly felt as such by the horse.

To those not accustomed to using this forward aid, it may take a little while to adopt it instinctively and to reject for ever the old method. Self-discipline and concentration, however, will do the trick and many advantages will be discovered. For one thing, the logic is so compelling. Furthermore, there is the great advantage that your aid, for so long as it is applied, will remain on the most sensitive part of the horse's barrel with the result that it can be that much lighter without being less effective.

It is worth giving a moment's thought to the logical development of this inward and forward aid when it is used to maximum effect. As the firmness of the forward action is increased so, because of human anatomy, will there be a tendency for the toe to turn out a little and the heel to come into increased contact with the horse. When spurs are worn they also will ultimately come into contact, but only in a comparatively sensitive and kind manner. That is to say, the end of the spur will be drawn rather than pushed forward, against the lie of the hair and in the opposite direction to where it is pointing. In this way there is no possibility of the horse being pricked or bruised by the spur. He will not resent it or be frightened of it. It will only come into action when and if the horse has been a little slovenly in responding to the normal leg pressure and then without any change in the type or direction of the aid. Confidence and mutual understanding will be maintained. And should positive resistance or disobedience by the horse ever call for a degree of punishment, the use of the spur in that manner in that sensitive part will be extremely effective while remaining relatively harmless and kind.

Not the least valuable result from the adoption of the forward squeeze for going forward is that for all normal purposes the rider and the horse can settle down to work on the clear understanding that the rider's leg will never be moved backward from the basic position except for either positively moving the quarters to one side or passively preventing them from moving to one side when such movement is undesirable. This will be found to be a useful simplification of the language. The exceptions will be restricted to flying changes in canter and to correctly elevated piaffes, neither of which will cause us any inconvenience when those stages are reached. In all other respects total consistency can and should be practical. In this way the leg remains more still, the horse is not disturbed by uncertain movements by the rider, and the rider sits more correctly with a long and uninterrupted leg contact.

We have made rather a long digression into some of the techniques of riding, but they are matters that will be constantly in our mind as we go about our daily routine, and the more firmly they are established into our system, the more smoothly shall we progress towards our goal. All the work we are now doing is extremely simple, and it is consequently an excellent moment to correct and improve our simple aids.

Work in walk and trot

Our work for at least the first two months of this three-month phase will consist almost entirely of walking and trotting, the former being carried out of a long or even loose rein to allow the horse as much free-dom of his neck and shoulders as possible as an inducement to him to lengthen his stride, and the latter as free as possible but always on a light contact. The background to it all is that the horse shall grow accustomed to carrying the rider without losing the balance he has already acquired on the lunge. He must be encouraged to lengthen and slightly lower his neck at this stage to help him take and keep the contact while not in any way restricting the still quite weak muscles in his back. He must not, however, be allowed to lie on the hand, and the rider must be prepared to sacrifice a degree of control in order to ensure that this does not occur. So long as the paces remain active and the momentum is maintained in the frequent downward transitions, the horse will gradually improve in his balance and in doing so will lose any need to use the rider's hand as a support. It is a good thing to make frequent tests of this factor by releasing and retaking contact, or stroking the neck, either with one or with both hands, which also has the effect of calming and reassuring the young horse and increasing his own self-confidence.

Only very large circles should be attempted, care being taken to exercise sufficient forethought to avoid sudden emergency turns that might cause temporary collapse of balance and rhythm. If such a turn is necessary, for example, when riding along a country track, it is better to come back to a walk and then to resume the trot after the corner has been negotiated.

It should not be thought that it will be safe and satisfactory to use the sitting trot all the time. It should not be attempted for at least the first six weeks, and then only for ten or a dozen strides at the most to test the feel. The feel the sensitive rider will be looking for is the one that indicates that the horse is in no way inconvenienced or unbalanced or knocked out of his rhythm by the sudden unbroken contact with the saddle. In trying this out the rider must remember to pay particular attention to the suppleness of his own back. There should be the minimum of tension or bracing in his own back muscles so that with a good, free forward ripple in the lumbar region he will minimize any bumpy discomfort to the horse, his weight being carried well forward with the movement. These early experiments with the sitting trot are really critical, so the rider must approach them with humility about himself and sympathy for his young and inexperienced pupil. If the horse finds that his early experiences of carrying a rider cause him pain or discomfort to his back, he will quite naturally try to save himself by withdrawing his back away from the point of discomfort. That means that he will slightly hollow it, which would immediately begin to prohibit the growth of muscle and suppleness. The deliberate withdrawal of the back, accentuated by fatigue and weakness, may even end in the horse becoming permanently and visibly hollow-backed. The trainer, therefore, must never forget the need to consider the degree of strain he is imposing on his young horse's back by his own manner of riding and by the exercises he asks the horse to perform. Failure to do this may all too easily cause a degree of muscular pain which, together with the consequent mental resentment, will quite quickly induce a resistance that will plague both horse and rider for many years, if not permanently.

By the end of the first two months we can expect to have established a happy and confident relationship in which both parties increasingly enjoy a relatively carefree daily workout, whether it be in the home paddock or on quiet lanes and tracks. Every advantage should be taken of opportunities to work on hills, slopes or uneven ground to improve balance and to free the muscles and joints. Where no hilly ground is available, all the more trouble must be taken to ensure that the freedom is obtained by active and unconstrained work on the flat. We particularly want at this stage to aim at a happy atmosphere, with perhaps a slightly carefree approach to work, encouraging the young horse to stretch and use his body and limbs as much as possible.

The canter

The canter need not be introduced into the routine in any hurry, and certainly not until complete calmness and confidence have been established in trot. Any unsteadiness in the trot is almost certain to be exaggerated in the canter, which may also bring with it a certain excitability that will express itself in an unsteadiness in the head and mouth. If this is difficult to deal with without roughness the canter is best avoided until such time as the waywardness has been forgotten and worked out of the horse's mind by quiet work in the other two paces. When reintroduced it may be best to ask for just a very few paces at canter before bringing the horse back to the trot as gently as possible. Frequent repetitions of these transitions will leave the horse little time to think about the excitements or irritations of the canter, and he will probably soon forget about them and begin to accept that gait as calmly as the trot. That, at any rate, is what the trainer must strive for above all else at this stage, and he must be prepared to exercise great patience and not be upset if the achievement takes quite a long time. With many young horses there will be no problem at all, the horse working calmly at all three paces almost straight away. But there is no need to regard it as a crisis if some uncertainty does arise with the canter. Like many other problems that occur with the majority of horses, it can be confidently relied on to disappear in good time when, probably almost overnight, it will be gone.

Just as in the trot, in which the rider should keep the young horse's back as free as possible initially by always rising at that pace, so also at the canter he should try to sit as light in the saddle as possible, sitting well forward towards the pommel and ensuring that his own back is supple enough to absorb any tendency to bump. If he feels that the horse is resenting the pressure on his still-weak back muscles, so that the canter feels a little bumpy or humpy, it may even be wise to take all the weight off the saddle by standing in the stirrups so as to let the horse swing quietly along underneath and enjoy the movement without the unaccustomed irritation of a possibly not too supple rider on his sensitive back. A few weeks should be sufficient for the rider to win his acceptance in the saddle, particularly if by that time the horse has developed enough strength to permit him to sit at the trot, as will certainly be the case if the canter has initially been postponed for a month or so.

Turn on the forehand

If all is going well with these very basic matters, we can, perhaps in the third month, begin to introduce our horse to some of the interesting exercises that will form part of his education. Nothing advanced,

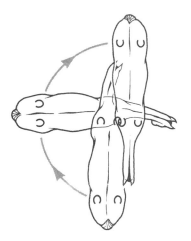

Figure 2

nothing complicated and nothing that might excite him at this stage, but just a few things that will make him think and realize that there is such a thing as induced co-ordination of movement. Later, we shall find that co-ordination of movement is displayed and achieved most effectively by the various forms of lateral movement and here, while the educational process is just beginning, we can quite safely take the first tentative and gentle steps. In fact we have already taken them, even before we climbed on to the horse's back, when we taught our pupil his early stable manners for which he was required to move over in his box so that he could be groomed on both sides or just to keep out of the way when his bedding was being cleaned. At first he will not have had any idea what he was being asked to do and will probably have wandered aimlessly round and round the box becoming more and more bewildered. So he had to be taught, and this was quite quickly done by tying him up by his headrope and then encouraging him to move his quarters in the required direction by pressure, or perhaps little prods, with the hand applied about half-way back along his rib-cage. As soon as he moved his feet in order to take his body away from the hand pressure, he will have been thanked with the voice and patted on the neck with the other hand. Then a few more accommodating steps followed by more pats and perhaps a tit-bit or two and the lesson will have been learned, subject only to repetition and improvement on subsequent days and in both directions. That is the first lesson in lateral work of which the most important aspect is the control and mobilization of the quarters. And that early lesson will soon become a matter of daily domestic routine that will never be forgotten and will form the basis of many more interesting things.

In the stable we shall have been content to let the horse swing his whole body, and all four feet, round an arc based on the ring to which his rope was tied, though even so the hind feet will have taken rather bigger steps than the forefeet. But now that we are on his back and have begun to acquire some mutually acceptable control of the front end of the horse by means of the bridle and the reins, we can convert the moving-over exercise into a true and controlled turn on the forehand. We should realize that it may and probably will take us two or three days to get a reasonably satisfactory result, so we must not be in a hurry. It is not a very easy movement for any horse to perform well or to understand at first, and we must therefore allow plenty of time and determine not to get involved in any sort of struggle. At the same time we need not be afraid of attempting this movement once the young horse has come to accept our overall control without fuss. The turn on the forehand imposes no sudden or great physical strain on any part of the horse, and it is performed quite slowly and quietly with plenty of time for both horse and rider to think about and feel what they are each doing. The action can be carried out a step at a time, or pushed through to three or four steps, stopped and restarted and so forth. Calmness can and must be maintained. Should the horse show any tendency to rein back, even if ever so little, he should be urged forward in a straight line before the turning movement is recommenced for another step or two.

With this exercise of the turn on the forehand we are taking a decisive step forward in educating the horse to understand and respond to the increasingly sophisticated and infinitely variable language of the aids. Up to now we shall have done little more than convert the psychological appeal of the voice to the primitively physical indication of the rein or the leg that he should go on, stop or turn a little to the right or the left. In the first two instances he has felt both reins or both legs with unmistakable meaning, and in the latter he will hardly have been able to avoid following the indication of the opening or direct rein to alter his course. But now it is time to explain that we expect him to be able to pay attention and respond to two quite different aids at the same time. These ideas will come as a surprise to almost every young horse, and we shall feel that surprise and initial incomprehension clearly expressed in his awkward and possibly rather flustered reactions. But we shall soon overcome these difficulties provided we act with the appropriate patience and tact. As with every other new lesson, the rider must first be clear in his own mind about the aids that he is going to employ. That is to say, he must clearly understand the simple mechanical effect of the various aids at his disposal and must use only those that are appropriate to the result that he wishes to obtain. It is not enough that he should have a rather vague idea that under certain circumstances he should pull this rein or apply that leg. Only if he truly understands the mechanics of the aids will he be able to apply them judiciously and with discretion in accordance with the infinitely variable circumstances that will confront him.

As with every other lesson, we approach it from the easiest possible direction, and we make sure that there is a logical and therefore easily understood link with a previous lesson that has been well absorbed. Many things, for horse and for rider, are linked to this first simple lesson in lateral work, the turn on the forehand.

In the turn on the forehand the horse has to move his quarters around the more or less fixed pivot of his forefeet. In order that the rider may retain proper control, the horse's neck and head should remain in their original straight alignment with the trunk, although a slight flexion of the poll in the direction to which the head is moving, for example to the left if the quarters are going to the right, is desirable and helpful as will be explained later. To achieve this reaction from the young horse, the rider's leg aids will present no great problem as they will merely have to give the same message to the horse as the pushing hand did in the stable exercise of moving over, but with the addition that now we can use the leg on the opposite side to limit or control any excess movement should that be necessary. The main pushing leg is used well back behind the girth so as to make its intention perfectly clear to the horse, the pressure being applied only with the flat inside portion of the leg, avoiding any tendency to turn the toe out in order to use the back of the heel. That way the horse will not feel threatened and will remain in a better state of mind to think quietly about the rather strange manoeuvres that he is being asked to perform.

The correct use of the two reins is rather less simple than the use of the legs, though obviously the two aids cannot be effectively co-ordinated unless they are equally well understood. For the purpose of simple steering, there are five basic but different effects that can be applied through the reins. These will be explained in detail at the end of this chapter but for the moment it will be sufficient to mention only the one that we shall require in teaching our horse the turn on the forehand. It is called, a little ponderously, the indirect rein of opposition behind the withers. There is no need to be alarmed or put off by all those words because in point of fact they explain in admirable detail just how the rein effect is achieved.

We will assume that we are going to make a right turn on the forehand, which means that the quarters will have to move from right to left in a circular manner around the forehand, the head and neck moving from left to right. We start by creating movement in a mainly forward direction, and we then block that movement with the right rein only. That is the meaning of the word 'opposition'. There should be no backward pull, the blocking action merely opposing forward movement on that side of the horse. But the left side of the horse remains free and unopposed, so the movement that we have initially created will naturally tend to escape in that direction. The use of the right rein is therefore resulting in movement to the left, which is why it is referred to as 'indirect'. We cannot use the left rein to produce the same result because it would tend to make the horse turn his head in that direction which would be undesirable in this exercise and would interfere with the desired movement of the quarters. We must be careful that the line of the opposing right rein does not cross the axis of the horse in front of his withers as that would powerfully hinder our efforts. But if the line of opposition is maintained well behind the withers it will create a mechanical effect on the whole body of the horse that is complementary to that created by our pushing right leg. That is to say, the quarters will move away to the left. So we have a situation in which the right leg and the right rein are working together to produce exactly the kind of turning movement that we want. In short, we are using lateral aids, the rein and the leg on the same side being predominant and the leg and rein on the opposite side being used only to control or moderate the movement as may be necessary.

It is well worth while taking a lot of trouble to perfect this movement of the turn on the forehand. It is sometimes regarded as a rather primitive affair that can be missed out of the curriculum or, once done, can be quickly forgotten as something that was only useful in the beginning. That attitude is mistaken and indicates a failure to understand the value of good foundation work. Rather, it should be the trainer's aim to be able to exercise and control each and every part of his horse. In that context nothing is more important than the quarters and few things exercise and loosen the quarters more effectively than the turn on the forehand and the more advanced but directly related movements such as circles performed on two tracks with quarters out. The turn on the forehand has the inestimable advantage that it provides a method of demanding something quite difficult from the horse from a very slow pace, almost a halt, so that there is little or no element of excitement, and the horse and rider together have plenty of time to work out the problems and overcome the initial difficulties. Every horseman will know how extremely frustrating it is to try to open or shut a gate from the back of a horse that has not learnt this relatively simple lesson. There is no shortage of very good reasons for teaching this lesson early and then keeping it well polished up. It is necessary always to go back to square one as a frequent check.

It is not necessary at this early stage in the training to worry about the correct co-ordination of the steps of the front legs with those of the all-important hind legs. We can be content so long as the hind legs move freely to the side away from our pushing leg, there being no resistance in the neck and mouth. To confirm obedience and a full understanding we can later on alternate the movement first to one side for, say, a quarter of a turn, then back in the other direction for half a turn, and finally back for a quarter of a turn to the original alignment. And as the horse's dexterity progresses, each improvement should be quickly and generously rewarded with pats on the neck.

After a couple of weeks we should have obtained a sufficient degree of easy obedience of the quarters to the rider's leg at the halt to make it possible to proceed confidently to the next step in lateral work. We can move the quarters at the halt, so we now begin to move them on the move, at the walk. The easiest way to do this is to take the horse off a straight track on to a small half circle of about six metres in diameter, and as we do so to apply precisely the same lateral aids that we used for the turn on the forehand. We make a right half-circle, gently applying a degree of indirect opposition behind the withers with the right rein and pushing the quarters outwards and off the track made by the front legs with our well drawn back right leg. In this way, using a fairly small half circle, we make use of the natural tendency of the horse to let his quarters swing outwards on any tight bend, in order to help teach him to obey our pushing leg when on the move. The walk should be kept very slow so that there will be no question of the young horse losing his balance or his confidence. There is seldom any difficulty in learning this exercise provided that the work at the halt has been thoroughly absorbed. But it is nevertheless an important step on the road we are following, in particular because it increases the young horse's confidence in his ability to respond to unexpected or abnormal demands made upon him by the rider.

Forward leg response

In the latter stages of our Phase 2 training period, or the first three months of ridden work, we should be giving priority over all other considerations to the lesson of forward leg response. The young horse must, and I repeat must, by this stage be willing to move forward with increased vigour and without any hesitation to an increased pressure of both legs applied in their normal position immediately behind the girth.

The vital need to establish forward leg response at this early stage is due to the fact that from now on we shall be gently but steadily increasing the difficulty of the lessons we shall be teaching. The biggest danger to be guarded against in all of them will be the tendency for the horse to lose his momentum, his forwardness, in his efforts to grapple with the problems of the exercises. We must always be able instantly to regain the forward urge that is at the root of all equitation. We shall not be able to regain and maintain that controlling factor under difficult circumstances unless the lesson is deeply and permanently instilled into the mind of the horse so that we can rely upon his unquestioning co-operation in this special respect. We have to remember that the response we are seeking is not and cannot be a purely physical reaction to the pressing of a certain button. It is very largely a matter of communicating with the horse's mind. We have to win his interest and mental response, the aids we use being merely the language with which we communicate.

The strike-off

Depending on the temperament and on the natural athletic ability and balance of the young horse, it could well be that we shall have done very little canter work during the lungeing phase and again very little during the first month or so of Phase 2. But by the latter stages of Phase 2 we should expect a quiet and fairly free canter, as much as possible on a long or perhaps loose rein, to have become an accepted part of the regular routine. Calmness is important in all the work, but it is especially so with the canter. If the horse shows any tendency to become excited or to play about with the bit or to pull, we should only adopt that pace occasionally for very short spells alternated with walk and trot. Some horses take quite a long time, perhaps even a year, before they can accept the canter as calmly as the other two paces.

Gradually, the canter will settle, and we can begin to polish it up. At the very outset we should not worry about which leg the horse strikes off on, just pressing him forward and using the vocal command that he came to understand on the lunge. We should avoid taking him around curves or corners of any kind in counter canter, but rather bring him back to a trot or walk if he happens to be on the inappropriate leg. But just as soon as we can canter quietly and confidently on demand, we can begin to teach the lesson of the strike-off on a prescribed leg. This can usually be done without much difficulty by the use of a little tact and guile. First, the rider must make up his mind without any shadow of doubt precisely what aids he intends to use for the strike-off so that he can start as he intends to continue. Of the various schools of thought the author would strongly advise the use of the more conventional method which depends on the predominant use of the inside leg, used with a distinctly forward action on to the girth, preceded by a slight but distinct withdrawal to the rear of the outside leg which should not exert any pressure whatsoever beyond the normal light contact. This withdrawal of the outside leg serves the dual purpose of helping to keep the horse straight and of warning the horse that that leg is out of action and not the one that will be asking for the strike-off.

To begin with, the canter should be asked for at some moment when the horse is most likely to lead with the desired leg, such as on a bend or circle in the appropriate direction. Then, with luck, a chosen strike-off can be made to coincide with the appropriate aid and a start has been made to link the two together in the mind and memory of the horse. As soon as the coincidence happens it must be followed immediately by pats on the neck and a quiet change back to the walk for a few minutes to let the idea sink in. It can then be repeated several times in the same way until the lesson is, at least for the day, reasonably well established.

Of course it will not always work out quite as easily as that. For all sorts of reasons, such as physical imbalance or some preconceived idea of his own, the horse may strike off on the wrong leg, and this may well be repeated several times. If this happens the rider must on no account make any sort of scene or try to offer any sort of reprimand. Action should be confined solely to regaining the trot as quickly and as quietly as possible before trying again as soon as suitable conditions of direction, pace, ground and so on can be arranged. Sooner or later the strike-off will come on the expected leg and, if the aid has been correct and consistent, we shall be in the clear. If we can repeat the exercise correctly twice we would be well advised to call it a day and walk the horse back to the stable. It is best to postpone dealing with the opposite leg until the next day to avoid risk of confusion. Take one leg each day until both are well confirmed, and then they can be mixed.

It should go without saying that the rider must avoid any temptation he may feel to obtain the desired strike-off by throwing his own weight about, leaning over to the side, or nudging with his outside leg. These things will tend to upset the horse and the latter will also tend to make him go crooked into the canter. The correct seat and aids combined with patience will do the trick and be the foundations of further trouble-free progress. A distinct opening of the rein on the side of the desired leading leg will often be very helpful if given in direct conjunction with the inside leg aid.

Rein aids

The reins, of course, are an immensely important and powerful part of the rider's equipment, and they are capable of being used in an almost infinite variety of ways and strengths. Inevitably, they are in nearly constant use, and unless very great care is applied to them, they can all too easily do more harm than good and can even counteract or wreck all other work.

The great power and importance of the reins arises from the fact that they are, of all the aids, by far the most directly mechnical in their application. The rider cannot invent his own language for the reins as, to a considerable extent, he can for his legs, his whip and perhaps even his weight. If he smacks his horse smartly on the ribs with his whip there is no purely mechanical reason why the horse should go forward or faster. That he probably does so is the result mainly of psychological factors connected with pain and fear. But if the right rein is pulled hard enough the horse must sooner or later turn to the right for mechanical reasons that are far stronger in the last resort than any mental urge he may have to go to the left. So with two reins more or less permanently in play and capable of being used in a mutually contradictory manner, the opportunities for their misuse by a careless or ignorant rider are clearly enormous. And misused they certainly are, all too frequently. It follows also that a lack of knowledge and understanding of their subtle potentialities will deprive the rider of a considerable amount of his own ability to influence his horse.

As we have recognized, there are an almost infinite variety of possible rein aids, but for all practical purpose they can all be regarded as falling into one of just five groups which are usually called the five rein effects. These are, respectively:

1. The direct, or open rein.
2. The indirect rein.
3. The direct rein of opposition.
4. The indirect rein of opposition in front of the withers.
5. The indirect rein of opposition behind the withers.

From the titles, two words may need special explanation. The word 'indirect' means that the rein has its main influence towards the opposite side of the horse. The word 'opposition' means that the rein is applied in such a way as to oppose forward movement, though without any backward pull.

Provided those definitions are remembered, these five rein effects can be easily understood and memorized from Fig. 3 (overleaf) which also indicates some of the main purposes for which each rein effect is commonly or likely to be used, though it must always be remembered that no one rein is ever used in isolation. Each rein will always complement the other in some way, according to the circumstances and problems of the moment, either to endorse or to moderate the effect of the predominant rein. They must, of course, never contradict each other.

One very valuable result of a clear understanding of these irrefutable and inescapable aspects of the use of the reins is that it will make the rider very much quicker to spot when he is, by using his hands in an incorrect way, actually making things difficult for himself and for his horse. One quite common bad habit of this nature is when a rider tries to maintain a correct bend to the right, when doing a right half pass, by taking his right hand across the withers to the left. A glance at diagram four will show how muddling and difficult it must be for the horse. In the diagram, the single arrows show the direction of the rein effect, the broad arrows the mechanical effect produced on the horse, given some degree of impulsion.

The amount of movement required in practice by the rider's hand is much slighter than may appear from the diagrammatic explanation. The more advanced the state of training, the slighter and more invisible

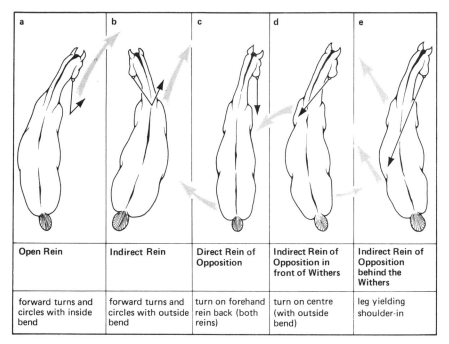

a	b	c	d	e
Open Rein	**Indirect Rein**	**Direct Rein of Opposition**	**Indirect Rein of Opposition in front of Withers**	**Indirect Rein of Opposition behind the Withers**
forward turns and circles with inside bend	forward turns and circles with outside bend	turn on forehand rein back (both reins)	turn on centre (with outside bend)	leg yielding shoulder-in

Figure 3   *Rein effects*

will be the movement. But at the same time the rein effects assume a greater and greater importance until, in the opinion of the French masters, only the reins are used to control direction of movement including all lateral work, while the legs are concerned only with activity and impulsion. That stage of training is not far from the sublime and is certainly far beyond the scope of this book, although the seeds of it can and should be sown during the first two years of training.

Note. The diagrams in Fig. 3 show the inevitable and mechanical effects of one rein only, used by itself.

CHAPTER EIGHT

Riding to the Bit

Phase 3 (Months 7–9)

Transitions. Canter. To the bit. Impulsion. Leg-yielding.
Supple bends. Half-halts. Trot to canter. Engagement of the quarters.

As we arrive at the end of Phase 2 and enter Phase 3, the second three-monthly period of ridden work, we should be well advised to pause to take stock of what we have achieved during those first six months of the educational process, three of them devoted primarily to work on the lunge and three to the most elementary forms of ridden work. In doing so it may come as a shock to realize that the horse has probably not yet fully recaptured the same standard of impressive dexterity, carriage and action that we had before our eyes towards the end of the lungeing period. That is to be expected and need cause no anxiety. On the contrary, it should be a salutary reminder of the severity of the burden that we impose on a young horse by sitting on his back. This will help us not to become impatient when our horse seems incapable of keeping a straight line, or flounders round a large twenty-metre circle when we have seen him float easily around the much smaller lungeing ring. The fact is that it takes a long time for the youngster to develop the extra strength and dexterity that will permit him to make the necessary adjustments to the balance he has already acquired when going solo, and we must make allowance for this process.

Our main object will have been to arrive at this point with a well-established understanding about going freely forward on straight lines with a light contact of the rein. Almost all our efforts and hopes will have been concentrated on that one aspect during Phase 2, and we should not have been unduly concerned about balance or the general posture of the horse. We shall have left him for the time being to work that out for

Active and forward. Dr Reine Klimke on a five-year-old Westphalian, Notturno, in working trot.

himself which he will certainly have been able to do to some extent provided we have not interfered with him through the reins.

It is not wise to try to reduce the length of Phase 2, even though circumstances and lack of good lungeing facilities may have forced us to cut the lungeing period and so begin the ridden work at an earlier date than was scheduled. That would only have resulted in the horse being less well prepared and ready for ridden work, and he will have needed more time under the saddle before he is ready to move on to Phase 3. In any case, if we are not reasonably satisfied with his willingness and ability to go forward calmly and with correct paces, we must be prepared to postpone Phase 3 for a little longer and spend the time working to correct what is wrong. But it is unnecessary to expect or try to insist on perfection at this or at any other stage. If we do that we shall not make progress, because true perfection is never attainable.

So how, it may be asked, can we be sure that we are adequately prepared? We can, if we wish, ask advice from some respected friend, but on the whole perhaps a little honest heart-searching is the best method, combined with a check on our own written programme. If we can then honestly give ourselves a grading of about seventy per cent, or fairly good, for the work we have been doing, then we can confidently push on. And because we are always, always recapitulating, the things we have found difficult in earlier phases will continue to improve in the future.

Nevertheless, we must realize that a certain minimum standard of performance at all stages is essential for the horse to be physically and mentally able to tackle more advanced work, and that standard is certainly not lower than sixty per cent. To try to advance from a point below that minimum is to court trouble and disaster if only because most riders will then be tempted to try to force their horses, with rough rein and leg aids, to do what they find too difficult and even painful. That way leads to resentment, insensitivity, sourness and disillusionment. Perhaps this problem can be summed up by saying that we want to be sure that at all times we have the feeling that our progress is open-ended, that it contains a momentum that will carry it on to further things, and that we can always feel the seeds of more difficult activities beginning to germinate inside the womb of the rider/horse relationship. If we cannot genuinely sense these feelings all the time, then we are probably on the wrong track: we are in some sort of a dead-end, and we should call for some help.

However, sooner or later we must come to the point where we feel confident about what we have done so far, and we can begin to concentrate our minds on the contents and problems of our Phase 3 programme. There is no feeling of any sudden or alarming change of style because of course we shall have been keeping this and the subsequent parts of our schedule well in mind from the very beginning so that we shall at all times be working within an overall perspective. What we have now to do is to speed up the work just a little so as to be able to introduce the new factors.

Engagement of the quarters

The concept of the engagement of the quarters is one that will increasingly concern us throughout our work, so it will be as well to be clear about it from the start. The theory presents no special difficulty, however difficult it may be to practise. Quite simply, by engaging the quarters we mean that we want to bring them into closer relation and co-ordination with the rest of the horse. By making them work harder, and provided we restrain any tendency to increase the speed, the quarters will naturally tend to catch up with the forehand. They will come a little further underneath the mass, shortening ever so little the base line between the front legs and the back legs, thus causing the hind legs to carry a greater proportion of the total weight than they would or could have done when they were further out behind. But in order to do this the horse must have a degree of roundness and suppleness in his back. The effort to engage his quarters more closely will be felt by him chiefly in the muscles of the loins, behind the saddle, and if those muscles are not strong and supple enough to take the strain he will never be able to engage himself, no matter how actively we urge him forward. In that case the horse will probably try to escape the physical discomfort he is feeling by raising his head so as to get off the bit and hollow his back, thus making engagement actually impossible. But we need not anticipate this problem provided that the conformation of the loins and hocks is sound and that we gave our horse the chance to build up the muscles by the appropriate work earlier on the lunge.

To the bit

By far the most important factor at this stage is to begin, not too suddenly but definitely to begin, to put the young horse to the bit. That means that we must, slowly but progressively, begin to control the length of the frame in which the horse moves and to teach him that he can and must continue to be active throughout his body within the controlled frame and without losing any of the free forward urge that has already become his habitual way of going. Indeed, the forward urge should gradually become more and more pronounced and firm as his capacity to control and co-ordinate it increases with the development of his physical strength, suppleness and agility. But progress in this matter must be gradual and must proceed hand in hand with the horse's ability to stretch the top line of his body and neck, to flex the joints of his hind legs, and to develop an upward and forward swing through the muscles of his back, despite the weight of the rider.

One way of explaining what we want to achieve would be to hold a moderately stiff riding whip with one end in each hand. So long as no pressure is exerted by the hands beyond that which is necessary only to hold the whip horizontally in the air, the whip will remain stretched to its full length with a slight tendency to sag in the middle. If we then exert just sufficient pressure to make it possible to counteract the tendency to sag and convert it into a very slight upward bend or arch, we shall be seeing and feeling something similar to the effect we want to achieve in our horse in this third phase. We want to be able to hold the spine and the muscular part of his back between our hands at one end and the pressure from his own hind legs at the other in much the same way as we were holding the whip, only then we had to use our second hand to substitute for the hind legs of the horse.

The increased pressure of the whip into the palm of the hand represents fairly accurately the impulsion that we now begin to ask for and to build up in the horse, though there is one big and very important difference between the analogy of the whip and the horse. With the former we can increase or decrease the pressure in the palm of the hand at will and with a high degree of control. But with the live horse we have to hand over the job done by the hand at the thick end of the whip to the horse's hind legs and quarters so that any increase we require in the pressure at the other end must emanate from the horse. We must never try to increase the pressure to shorten the frame by pulling backwards with the reins, as that would be in direct contradiction to the forward urge that we have been at such pains to develop and maintain. In practice it is always the back end of the horse, exemplified by the hand on the thick end of the whip, that must do the job of increasing the pressure at the front end of the frame, though only to the extent that it can be absorbed by the strength and suppleness of the back and neck muscles. If we try to proceed too fast and to exert a degree of pressure or impulsion from behind that is in excess of what the horse is capable of absorbing, the overstressed muscles will hurt and the horse will withdraw or hollow his back to avoid the pain. The whip has once more begun to sag, and in that position we can do nothing useful since the horse's conformation is such that muscle tone is immediately lost.

We should note that with true impulsion passing through an upward-swinging back, the top line of the horse is never shortened, though the length of the lower line, between the mouth and the hind feet, will be. The horse becomes like a bow, of which the string, between mouth and hind leg along the lower line, can be tautened and tuned, though not all at once, to a high degree of pitch and efficiency.

Not forgetting the analogies of the whip and the bow, we come back to real life with the horse. We have been teaching him to go freely forward and in doing so to stretch his back and neck structure so as to assume a slightly bow-shaped outline. Now we begin to take a rather firmer contact with the reins and the bit, but without permitting any reduction in the activity of the quarters. To achieve this, we have lightly to increase the demands of our own legs. Almost imperceptibly at first, this will have the effect of the horse pushing himself up to the bit which he finds is beginning to act like the hand at the thin end of the whip with its restraining effect. He will have learned not to be afraid of or to fight the bit, and so now his head will begin little by little to come closer to the vertical as the lower end, the muzzle, is restrained and the upper end is stretched forward by the impulsion from the quarters flowing forward through the back and neck to the poll. We must always strive to retain the feeling that we are lengthening and not shortening the neck, no matter how much the impulsion and the ultimate collection is increased. The reason for this is well illustrated in Fig. 4a which shows how the front and lower part of the spine within the thorax must drop still further if the neck is shortened, thus making it well-nigh impossible for the horse to shift weight back towards his quarters. With this manner of going he will remain in effect permanently on his forehand. Conversely, as the nose drops and the neck stretches, so the belly of the spine rises in the thorax, making it possible for the horse to learn to carry more and more of his weight with his quarters and loins (Fig. 4b).

It is just this process of combining a stretching forward of the neck with a willing lowering of the muzzle to a near vertical position that constitutes the putting of a horse to the bit. He must be prepared to flex his poll so as to drop his face line, and he must be willing to push himself forward into the rider's restraining hand. This is impulsion, flowing

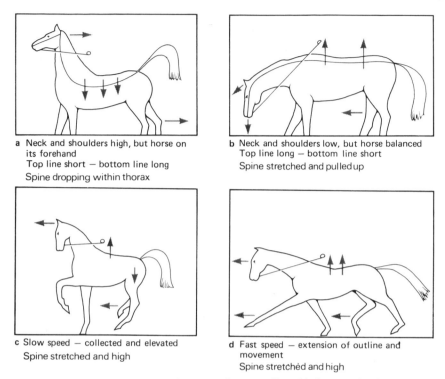

a Neck and shoulders high, but horse on its forehand
Top line short — bottom line long
Spine dropping within thorax

b Neck and shoulders low, but horse balanced
Top line long — bottom line short
Spine stretched and pulled up

c Slow speed — collected and elevated
Spine stretched and high

d Fast speed — extension of outline and movement
Spine stretched and high

Figure 4 *The horse's back and spine – the controller of balance and collection*

straight from the source right into the rider's hand, and with it the rider can do almost anything.

The chief danger, particularly at the beginning of this work, will be the temptation to pull the head into what we believe to be the right position. Such pulling will inevitably result in a shortening of the neck, the one thing we do not want. And in this connection it can be seen from (Fig. 4a) that the unwanted shortening will be all the more certain to happen if the horse has been carrying his head and neck too high in the first place. That is a vital reason why he must be made to stretch forward and down throughout Phase 2 and must retain the ability to do so when required in the future.

Being 'to the bit' is perhaps a more expressive description of what we want than the more conventional phrase of being 'on the bit'. In either case it must also be understood to imply a willingness by the horse to respond to the restraining action of the bit without loss of impulsion, and this can only occur if there is a supple flexion at his poll to provide the elastic joint wherein the impulsion and the restraint are combined. For example, where no poll flexion exists and the head is carried in the more or less natural position with the nose well in front of the vertical, the angle between the reins and the head will be so small that any restraining tension on the reins will flow not direct to the rider's hands and through the elbows to the seat, but straight back through the poll and neck. This poor angle inhibits the forward flow of impulsion and also tends to shorten the neck in the thoroughly undesirable way described in the previous paragraphs. With the head carried well in front of the vertical there can be no elastic restraining effect and so no true impulsion, no matter how fast the horse may be travelling. True, usable impulsion requires elastic, willing restraint, which in turn requires a willing flexion at the poll. These things cannot be divorced.

No excuse need be offered for going so fully into the related matters of flexion, impulsion and being to the bit. They need a lot of thought, and we shall make little further progress unless we have arrived at a clear understanding of what we are talking about when we use those terms. They must receive our constant attention from now on, though we must also remember that the more supple the horse becomes the lighter will the impulsion feel in our hands. It will be there and available to use as powerfully as ever we could wish, but the more it is absorbed by suppleness through all the muscles of the horse, the lighter can be the contact with the reins.

Suppleness

Longitudinally

Suppleness, therefore, becomes our next concern. Longitudinally, say from tail to head within the vertical plane, the horse will gradually supple himself as a natural result of flexion and impulsion provided he is to the bit. By now he must accept a proper poll flexion and be prepared to work in a fully on the bit position with his head quite closely approaching the vertical. But he must also be willing and able to stretch his head and neck forward and down towards the ground whenever we ask him to without fuss and without change of pace. And we should continue to ask him to do this quite frequently, particularly at the beginning as well as sometimes at the end or in the middle of the lesson. By doing so we are using the only method available to us of ensuring that we are not committing the unforgivable and fatal sin of spoiling the flexibility and resilience of the back. Every young horse starts life with a gloriously supple back. Some of that quality will inevitably be lost from one cause or another during his life-span and by nothing quicker than insensitive training. But the suppleness of the back is the *sine qua non* for all good work and comfortable riding, so it must be our constant concern to preserve that suppleness by every means at our disposal and constantly thinking about it from the horse's point of view. If we have done a spell of work at a sitting trot, for example, we should remember that we have been putting a lot of pressure on the back and making it work very hard. So we should ask and allow the young horse to do what we would do for ourselves under similar circumstances; we should stretch it in the opposite direction to where the strain has been exerted. The horse's lessons make demands on him that are very tiring to his muscles and to none so much as to the muscles of his back which will become very painful if we do not take steps to refresh them after periods of stress and to relax them before hard work begins.

Laterally

Lateral suppleness is also needed to complete the total requirement, and this has to be worked for in a different way. For this we must begin to ride large circles and smooth curves, at the same time teaching the horse to follow the opening or direct rein but also to listen to and obey the guidance of the rider's inside leg round which he must curve his body. He must learn, in short, not to cut the corner by letting his shoulders and forelegs fall in on the curve instead of following the line of the curve exactly between his nose and his hind quarters. Most young horses are sensitive enough to learn this quite quickly, provided they are not thrown off balance by being asked to turn too sharp a corner. It is mainly done by lengthening and slightly increasing the pressure of the inside leg on the girth while the outside leg helps to drive the horse forward round the corner and up to his bit. The outside leg, however, must also take position a little behind the normal place in order to guard against any tendency for the quarters to swing outside the line of the curve on to a wider track. The smallest tendency for that to happen will destroy any suppling that the corner might have achieved since the horse will, in effect, cease being longer on his outer side and shorter on his inner side. The combination of stretching and contracting the muscles on opposing sides is the chief beneficial effect of work on circles and curves, provided only that all four legs follow the same track. And, subject to the same proviso, the second most beneficial effect is the improvement it brings to the length and quality of the pace because the outer pair of legs have to take rather longer strides than they would at the same pace on a straight line, whereas the inner pair have to take rather shorter ones. These requirements can be studied in the accompanying diagram.

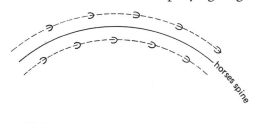

Figure 5
outside legs — long steps
inside legs — short steps
both legs of a diagonal in trot must conform

During this phase we should aim at being able to perform very good twenty-metre circles in the trot, the horse remaining bent, flexed on the poll, and on the bit with well-maintained impulsion. When working on the circle we must be sure that we ask for whatever bend and flexion we require with the inside hand only, while keeping a quiet and absolutely steady contact with the outer rein. The reason for this is that we want from the earliest stage to train the horse to work from our inside leg to our outside hand or rein, and to do that he must acquire confidence in the stability and dependability of that rein and hand.

The half-halt

The work on curves and circles is bound to accentuate problems of balance, and the maintenance of balance is a factor that will remain important to us throughout the training as it affects all horses no matter how talented they are or how advanced they become. Up to a point, but never sufficiently, the horse will try to help himself, but he needs encouragement and help to cope effectively with himself and his rider. We have to keep reminding him to make use of his quarters and loins to lighten the forehand which now carries most of the rider's weight, and we also have to introduce certain exercises that will help him to acquire the strength and the habit to do it. By far the most effective exercise for our purpose, and fortunately one that can be brought into play at virtually any moment on any occasion and at any pace, is the half-halt. This has always been something that is not easy to explain to those who do not already understand it as it is not a clearly defined movement in itself but rather a corrective or preparatory action. The half-halt, if properly executed, ensures that the horse is mentally alert and physically in a posture from which he is able to give of his best in whatever manner we may ask.

The half-halt is an action that has many degrees and subtle variations that can be used to suit the almost infinite variety of horse/rider circumstances that may occur. In essence it comprises an increase in the forward drive of the seat and legs and a quickly following lift of the hands combined with an increase in the restraining effect of the reins. The action of the legs and seat increases the activity of the hind legs, and the subsequent action of the hands prevents that activity resulting in an increase of speed, thus causing the activated hind legs to work further forward under the mass so that they are able to take more weight off the forehand without loss of impulsion. The horse is thus prepared for some improved or different performance. Finally, to complete the action of the half-halt, the restraining lift of the hands must not be retained but must change smoothly into a forward release, as it were to replace the horse on a level and enduring keel. As always, the most difficult part of the whole process for most riders will be to achieve the restraining effect of the reins without pulling backwards with the hands. It may help to think of the hands as moving a little bit forwards as they lift in order to follow the circumference of an arc that pivots round the bit, the reins always remaining lightly taut. The return of the hands to the normal position will naturally follow the same course in reverse.

The half-halt process has been particularly aptly described by General DeCarpentry and others as requiring the same action as the man who lifts a heavy stone from one step of a staircase and places it gently upwards and forwards on to the next higher step. The same initial bracing by the back and thighs; the same grip and lift with the hands; and the same gentle forward placement and release.

We must not expect the half-halt to be fully understood and effective when we first use it. It is bound to take several weeks at least and maybe several months, depending on the sensitivity, responsiveness and intelligence of the horse. There is no hurry, but we should certainly be able to obtain some appreciable results by the end of this phase, and these can then be improved on gradually until excellent effects can be felt in the horse with no visible action by the rider beyond, perhaps, an extra bracing of the back.

We cannot begin to employ half-halt processes until the horse has learned to respond to and obey the rider's leg immediately and freely when asked to go forward. The closing of both legs, but with some predominance of the inner leg, must obtain an immediate response in the form of unquestioning forward movement. That matter of leg response was firmly established, or should have been, in the first three months of ridden work, and now we can see why that lesson was so important. To improve the horse's balance we have to employ half-halts. The half-halt cannot be effective, in fact cannot happen, without that immediate leg response because that is the action that initiates the half-halt as was described in our definition. The second part of the process, the restraining action of the hands, cannot function until the increased impulsion has been provided. In practice it all happens extremely quickly, but the sequence of events must be correct or else we shall end by pulling back the front end which will result in a shortening of the neck and a hollowing of the back.

As soon as the half-halt process begins to be understood by the horse it should be employed very frequently and that can be interpreted, without being too precise, as meaning at least six times in the course of one full circuit of an arena. The proper use of half-halts involves considerable activity from the rider which the inexperienced person will find quite exhausting at first. The lazy rider will try to persuade himself that his horse is going perfectly well of his own accord, that at that stage he doesn't need any additional impulsion or balance, and that there is no point in getting at him or disturbing his calm and pleasant way of going. No doubt both parties will then get back to the stable without getting hot, but the overall progress made during the lesson will have been very small. It will be found in the end to be an unproductive approach to things and will bring with it stagnation and disappointing delays in the progress that we hope to make. So we drill and accustom ourselves to make use of half-halts whenever we feel there is just a little room for improvement in the activity and balance of our young horse, and whenever we know that we are about to ask him to do something a little more difficult.

Improving the canter

We must expect the canter circles to be more difficult for the horse and take longer to become balanced than those in the trot. It is only logical, therefore, that we shall be able to reduce the size of the trot circles before those of the canter, in which the horse will have a natural tendency to allow too much weight to fall on to his forehand, until he has learned to engage his quarters sufficiently to solve that problem. And when we feel a sensation of awkwardness in the canter on the circle, we should remember that the horse is again having to grapple with the problem that he first encountered in the trot of co-ordinating a stretching of his outside muscles with a contraction of the inner ones. The problem in the canter will be rather more difficult for him to solve owing to the asymmetry of that pace as compared with the perfectly symmetrical alternation of the diagonals in the trot. The counter canter on the circle will be more difficult still, and it will be unwise to attempt it on anything more difficult than quite short curves until the horse can canter comfortably on the true lead on circles as small as fifteen or even twelve metres in diameter.

If the canter was proving difficult by the end of Phase 2 we should begin now, in Phase 3, to make a determined effort to get it accepted by the horse as easily and calmly as he accepts the trot. As the trot itself steadies and improves, we should introduce more and more frequent transitions into the canter for perhaps ten or fifteen strides only before coming back again into a rising trot with a good pat on the neck. The horse should by now be able to carry the rider in sitting trot for quite frequent if fairly short periods without feeling fatigue or pain in his back, so we can then revert to sitting trot again, perhaps do a good and well-controlled twenty-metre circle and once again ask for a clear strike-off into the canter as we complete the circle. That way he will begin to think of the canter as something of a relief from the not inconsiderable effort of maintaining a proper bend round the trot circle and so enjoy the canter instead of regarding it as a pace that is both rather difficult and disturbing. We should also try to canter on a long rein to encourage him to stretch and to treat the pace as a relaxation to body and mind. Any tendency to rush on can probably be overcome by leading him, still on a long rein if possible, on to a large circle for one or two circuits before going back on to a straight line and reverting gently to a rising trot. This process can be repeated as necessary.

We may have thought it wise to keep our weight off the saddle in the canter for some or all of Phase 2, but now we should expect the horse to carry our weight provided we sit as lightly and supply as we can. We must keep our own back working with the swing of the movement or else we cannot expect the horse to do just that with his own back. The smallest degree of bumping from the rider at this sensitive stage will soon set up the habit of muscle contraction in the horse that may take a long time and great skill to eradicate later on.

The ramener

By the end of the first month of Phase 3 we should no longer be prepared to make any excuses for our horse being unable to work in trot
and canter, and also for very short periods at the walk, fully and properly
on the bit, accepting the bit with a flexed and supple jaw and poll, the
line of the head being close to the vertical. It may be that we should not
ask him to work within this frame for more than five or ten minutes
at a time without a spell of relaxation on a long rein for another five
minutes, but it should now be clearly agreed between horse and rider
that when serious work is called for it is done in that manner. If the early

Figure 6

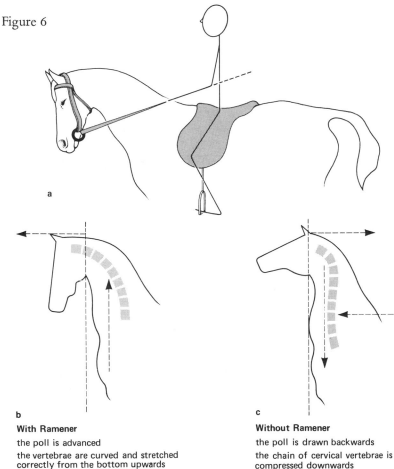

a

b
With Ramener

the poll is advanced

the vertebrae are curved and stretched
correctly from the bottom upwards

the neck is correctly carried from the
base upwards

c
Without Ramener

the poll is drawn backwards

the chain of cervical vertebrae is
compressed downwards

It flexes forwards at the lower part —
thus causing a ewe-neck
(Pigeon Throat)

education on the lunge in Phase 1 has been properly carried out, there should be no serious difficulty in arriving at this agreement.

The problem for the rider is to combine firmness with understanding and generosity and at the same time to be very much alert to anticipate and discourage the cunning efforts of the horse to break out of the discipline. This he will do by such means as dropping behind the bit on one or both sides; by trying to throw his weight against the rider's hand so as to pull him out of the saddle and so obtain a longer rein; or by trying to swing his quarters out of the straight so that he can no longer be asked for impulsion. There is no end to the tricks that an intelligent horse will discover and try to use. The rider, therefore, must be very well balanced himself; totally independent of his hands; relaxed in his shoulders, elbows and wrists so that he can feel and follow the slightest variation in his contact with the horse's mouth; and very determined that he will have it his way and not be beaten to it by the horse. He must always try to be one jump ahead. All the time he must also be riding the horse well forward so as to give him something to do that will occupy his mind as soon as he gives himself to the job. And the rider must be quick to express his appreciation by a pat on the neck every time the horse gives him two or three really good strides without any resistance in the neck or mouth. That pat on the neck is worth its weight in gold, but it should be delivered without immediately letting the horse escape and rest. That can follow after a few more steps – or, at a later stage, after a few more minutes – but at this stage it would be a mistake to let the horse think that three good strides is all that is wanted. He must come to think of it as the best way to get and to keep on getting pats and appreciative noises from the rider.

To work comfortably in the ramener position (or to the bit) the horse must have soft and flexible muscles at and below the poll and around the gullet. If we postpone for too long our demand that he shall adopt and work in this position, we are making it much harder for the horse as his neck and gullet muscles will have become stronger without becoming supple. That is why it is desirable to start work on this aspect as soon as we are satisfied that he has learned the lesson of going forward with freedom on request, provided only that his conformation and condition are such that he is capable of using his back. That must be a matter of judgement by the trainer or his advisers, but there should be no cause for worry with any horse of sound conformation with a good straight back that has been well grown, well lunged and well fed. Nevertheless, the ultimate aim remains clear, and it involves the fact that only when he works in the ramener, with a flexed and supple poll, will his back be free. Only when the back is free can the quarters come into full play and engagement. It is not sufficient for the face line to be at forty-five, twenty-five or even fifteen degrees from the vertical. At anything like those angles the muscles of the neck and back will remain too hard and his paces will suffer as also will the comfort and pleasure of the rider. We must ask for and be able to maintain without resistance a face-line angle of not more than about five degrees. Then we have somewhere to put the impulsion; then the blood begins to tingle with the anticipation of good things to come.

Further lateral work

Now, and even right at the beginning of Phase 3, we should begin to study the next lesson in lateral movement for which we have already done some very elementary preparatory work by practising the turn on the forehand and doing half circles with the quarters out in walk. In those two exercises the horse has learned to move his quarters in response to a light sideways pressure of one leg applied behind the girth and supported by a degree of opposition from the rein on the same side, the fifth rein effect. In other words, we have begun to mobilize and control the horse's quarters and that, in one way or another, is one of the most important aspects of horsemanship, because it is the quarters that make everything else tick.

We should now be sufficiently prepared to take this process one stage further into the altogether more sophisticated area where we learn to control the quarters at our will in faster paces and at the same time to co-ordinate the lateral movement of the quarters with a similar lateral control of the forehand. This would be quite difficult if it were attempted all at once, but we are making it much easier and comparatively simple by dealing with the problem in two stages, first the quarters and now the whole of the horse.

From now on, and with the exception of pirouettes and half pirouettes, all lateral movement implies going sideways as well as forwards, that is to say in a direction oblique or diagonal to the original alignment of the horse. It is possible but extremely difficult for the horse to move at right angles to his original alignment, and the danger of losing all impulsion and of causing the horse to damage his legs by knocking them are so great that such movement, called full pass, has no place in normal or classical dressage.

As with all other new lessons, we want to find and utilize the easiest and simplest way to introduce the horse to this new problem. We want somehow to make use of what he has already learned to help him to slip almost without knowing it into the new work. In that way each new step up the educational ladder is only a little one requiring no special or alarming effort that might make the horse anxious. If we can achieve progress in such a way, we shall be greatly helped by the fact that the horse will maintain and gradually increase his confidence in his trainer as well as in his own ability and cleverness.

Leg-yielding

With these principles in mind we now start to teach our horse the lesson of leg-yielding in which he is expected to move diagonally to one side while remaining quite straight from croup to poll except for a slight flexion away from the direction of movement. This is the simplest form of lateral movement of the whole horse and by far the easiest for him to perform. It makes less demands on him than other lateral work such as the half pass, because he does not have to perform it with any bend in his body. There is therefore no restriction of any sort on the muscles of one side as is bound to occur on the hollow side of a bend. In particular the main muscles of his quarters and of his shoulders and forelegs will have maximum freedom with which to learn to move in this new and unaccustomed manner.

Leg-yielding, like all other lateral movements, provides an additional and excellent means of stretching and suppling the horse in the lateral plane. It also adds very great interest and sense of pleasure to riding in all its forms and can be practised almost anywhere and at any time. Its chief purpose and benefit is that it teaches the horse to move his whole body freely to one side and away from the pressure of a leg.

To perform leg-yielding we again use lateral aids very similar to those which the horse has already come to understand and to respond to. He knows that he has to move away from a leg pressure behind the girth. We know that any activity by the horse that is controlled or modified by, for example, the right rein of opposition behind the withers, or fifth rein effect, will, as shown in Fig. 3e on page 90, cause the horse to move forward and sideways to the left. So if we now combine a pressure from our right leg behind the girth with the fifth rein effect on the same side, we are virtually bound to get some movement in the direction and of the kind that we want. If the horse is not positively disobedient to the leg he can hardly help himself. The logical power of the combined lateral aids will be compelling, and the horse will find himself doing something new that seems quite easy, not at all painful and for which he will get a pat on the neck.

Those are the main principles of leg-yielding, though there are one or two additional niceties that we will discuss as we take our horse through his first lesson. They will mainly concern the position of the rider's leg and the use of the supporting rein.

In addition to choosing leg-yielding as the next easiest lateral exercise, we need also to be sure that we introduce it to the horse in the simplest and most easily acceptable way: in circumstances that offer the greatest hope of success. For this purpose we will assume that we are working in an area where there is a well-worn track on which the horse is used to moving, be it in a rectangular manège or along the edge of a grass meadow. We are going to take this lesson at the walk to begin with as that is the pace which makes least demands on the balance of the horse and will give both horse and rider the most time to figure out how to deal with the numerous little problems and uncertainties that are bound to arise in the early stages. We shall start by walking along a line that is parallel to and only a few yards from the well-known and clearly visible track along the hedge or side of the arena. The centre line of an arena would do very well for our purpose.

Horses have excellent memories, are creatures of habit and have strong homing instincts, and we are going to make use of all those characteristics to assist us in this first lesson in leg-yielding. The centre line of an arena, or an invisible line on a grass field, is never a place on which a horse feels particularly at home and confident, but we can rely on his willingness to co-operate in moving a little sideways towards the old track that he can so clearly see just a few metres to, shall we say, his right. We ask for an active walk with the horse nicely on the bit and therefore paying attention, and as soon as we have it we quietly but rather firmly apply the two lateral aids – the left leg behind the girth assisted by the left rein of opposition behind the withers. But we never ride with one leg only or with one rein only; the right rein will be used with a slight opening effect to indicate to the horse the direction in which we want him to move, but mainly it will be concerned with supporting the left rein by ensuring that the bit is not pulled through the mouth to the left and, more immediately, that the neck is not bent to the left by the action of the left rein. We only want a slight flexion of the poll, otherwise the horse should remain straight throughout his length.

The right leg has to help maintain the original impulsion and also to prevent any tendency of the horse to fall away to the right too suddenly or too rapidly. We want the walk to be slow and deliberate to start with and to remain that way.

The first time we try it we must be well satisfied if we obtain just two or three clear steps of the movement to the right. If we get those willing steps, without being too fussy about the straightness of the neck, we must immediately release the left leg, and the opposing effect of the left rein, walk straight forward and make much of him. We can then repeat the movement several times hoping that, after four or five tries, we shall have moved quietly and smoothly all the way to the old track. We can be well pleased with the result and, with much patting, leave further work until the next day.

If we have encountered any serious difficulty, we should first check that the rider is applying his aids correctly. If the trouble persists we must look for some other reason, and the probability is that it will lie in the horse not having genuinely accepted and absorbed the earlier preparatory exercises. We should therefore immediately revert to going through all the earlier exercises once more and forget about the leg-yielding until we are satisfied that they can be executed whenever and as often as we wish without any resistance from the horse. Then, but only then, can we have another go at leg-yielding, using exactly the same method, and it will be most surprising if there is any further difficulty.

As soon as the lesson to the right has been accepted we can start at the beginning again with the lesson to the left, still in a walk. After two or three days, or a week at most if all is going well, we can without any special fuss make the same movement in trot, probably making it first in whichever direction proved most easy for the horse in walk. By the end of the second week we should have this simple lesson well established in both directions in walk and trot, the only remaining problems being to improve the impulsion and the straightness with which it is executed, and to maintain a lively but steady rhythm. We must especially try not to push and shove too much, but just to expect the appropriate response from the horse to a clear, firm but polite leg aid. That will surely be available if the earlier exercises have been well learned. And we must never forget the very true saying that if the pupil hasn't learned, the teacher hasn't taught.

Like all other lessons, we work our horse in leg-yielding on both reins, to right and to left, trying always to achieve the feeling that we can glide freely and effortlessly into the diagonal direction from the slightest but sustained pressure of the leg and without loss of rhythm from the preceding pace. We want it to free and supple the horse's limbs and joints, and we must for that very reason ensure that we also are supple and free, particularly in our loins and shoulders. If we become tense and fail to go with the movement with all that that entails, the horse will be inhibited from letting himself flow and will not enjoy the experience. If that happens we shall soon find him beginning to resist our requests and even to resent them altogether.

We can practise our leg-yielding on all sorts of occasions including when riding along roads or tracks, and from any straight line in a manège. But in the author's opinion it is inadvisable to teach or practise it by bringing the forehand in from the track on the long side of a manège and then proceeding somewhat in the manner of a shoulder-in. For one thing it is not so easy to get into the right position to start the movement in that way, and in trying to do so we shall probably disturb the horse's balance, rhythm and confidence just when we want to keep him perfectly poised and able to respond. If we try to ride the movement as a sort of false shoulder-in along the wall or track, we shall be inhibited from riding forward to improve impulsion for fear of losing touch with the track. On the other hand, moving into a leg-yield from a straight line as we have been doing requires no special preparation whatever beyond a little warning half-halt. We have to do nothing that will run any risk of upsetting the horse. We just walk or trot straight on and, when everything is right, we slide away diagonally. This way we also retain the invaluable ability to ride straight forward for a step or two if impulsion begins to fail and then quietly take the diagonal course again.

By far the most important reason for not practising leg-yielding along the side of the manège is that we shall very shortly be starting to teach an apparently similar but essentially different movement along that very track. I refer, of course, to the quite difficult but vitally important exercise of the shoulder-in. The difference between the leg-yield and the shoulder-in will become clear when we discuss the latter in the next chapter. Sceptics may say that a leg-yield is only a bad shoulder-in. It is, of course, much more than that both in intention and in execution, but there are similarities and the last thing we want to do at this stage is to let our horse acquire any preconceived ideas about the more difficult of the two exercises before we begin to teach it in the correct way. We do not want to have to unravel those ideas before we can start to inculcate the right ones. So we will have nothing to do with leg-yielding in a shoulder-in position along the perimeter track of a manège, at least until we have reached a much more advanced state of education. Meantime, we continue to practise and perfect pure leg-yielding in order to increase suppleness and freedom of movement, to increase obedience and attention, to improve balance and, by no means least, to bring the horse's education and understanding of the aids to a point from which he will have no difficulty in taking the next step up. For the latter purpose leg-yielding has great value and importance as a preparatory exercise.

During Phase 3, and certainly by the end of it, we should take a lot of trouble to ensure that the transitions from trot to canter are thoroughly prompt and reliable. The horse should by now step into the canter immediately on the aid, without coming off the bit and without any significant change in his activity. He should not slow down and he should not go in a faster tempo. He should quietly continue with the same sort of dialogue with his rider but in canter instead of trot. And the same should apply to the transitions from canter down to trot although they may be a little more difficult. In either case we should avoid asking for the new gait until we have the previous one in satisfactory balance and degree of impulsion. And in either case the transition must be ridden forward into the hand, and never from the hand backwards to the seat. That is much easier to say than to do, but it must be practised and accomplished if we hope to make real progress from one stage to another and into more and more difficult movements.

It will be advisable throughout this phase to include at least one lunge lesson as part of the weekly programme. It helps to vary routine and to keep the horse interested; it maintains and freshens up discipline and co-operation between horse and trainer; it gives the trainer a clear picture of physical progress; and above all it does wonders in keeping the paces loose, fresh and long. Both parties will get pleasure from the experience and it should not be neglected. No other work will be necessary after thirty minutes or so on the lunge.

CHAPTER NINE

End of the First Year
Phase 4 (Months 10–12)

Walk to canter. Shoulder-in. Serpentines. Canter changes.
Rein-back. 15 m trot circles.

Once again, as we find ourselves at the point of departure of a new phase
in our programme we must spare time to take a very sober and critical
look at what we have done and achieved up to this date. If there have
been no interruptions or setbacks from the weather or from illness there
is no reason why we should expect to be found wanting when judged
against our set target of between sixty and seventy per cent proficiency
in each part of the scheduled work. The fact that we have set a clearly
defined though restricted schedule for each phase will have helped us to
keep on the 'straight and narrow' and to concentrate on the essentials.
It will also make it easier to spot the errors when and if things seem to be
going awry, so that we can go back more quickly to pick up the threads
where they broke.

We are now approaching the point where we have so much on our
plate that we shall simply not have time to practise everything every day.
We shall soon have to begin to plan the daily ride in such a way that each
lesson to be worked on will be covered perhaps every other day, with
only the basic essentials being improved every day. There will be nothing
wrong with doing that because all horses have excellent memories and
very often show that they benefit in their ability to do some difficult
thing after a day's quiet meditation. So we plan certain exercises for
today and others for tomorrow, and then we find that they fit together
quite nicely when required.

A good shoulder-in. Miss Farlow on Snap Happy.

Shoulder-in

One of the first things to begin thinking about in this new Phase 4, the last three months of the first year of training, will be the shoulder-in. The eighteenth-century Frenchman de la Guérinière has been called the father of modern classical equitation and the shoulder-in, which he invented, has been his most important and valuable legacy. Although widely used in dressage displays and quadrilles and even in some high-level competitions, the shoulder-in is not in itself a spectacular or a particularly difficult movement, although it is intricate and not easy to perform accurately. But its value is beyond question and lies in the qualities it develops and in the remarkable degree of control that it bestows on the rider once it has been mastered by the horse and himself. It is, for this latter reason, no exaggeration to say that the shoulder-in contains the seeds of nearly all the more difficult movements that follow, including the canter pirouettes for the very advanced horses.

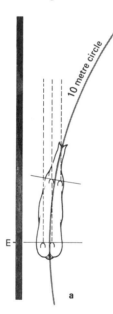
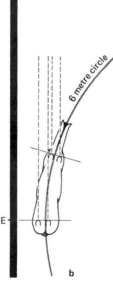
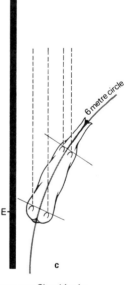

Correct Shoulder-In
horse bent for 10m circle
quarters square
3-tracks
only forelegs crossing

Correct Shoulder-In
horse bent for 6m circle
quarters square
4-tracks
only forelegs crossing

Incorrect Shoulder-In
horse bent for 6m circle
quarters twisted (not square)
4-tracks
fore <u>and</u> hind legs crossing

drawn to scale

Figure 7

Before making any effort to teach the shoulder-in we must be crystal clear in our mind about exactly how the movement should be carried out and what it is intended to achieve. So let us take a long look at the diagrams which will show the correct form of the movement as well as some of the chief faults to guard against.

In Fig. 7a, the correct shoulder-in, the first thing to notice is that the horse's quarters continue to move straight down the track as they did before the movement began. To underline this point, which is of very great importance if we are to obtain the full benefit from the movement, we can see that the line drawn through the two hip bones remains at or almost at right angles to the track or wall of the manège. In Fig. 7c we can see that the quarters have turned so that the quarters are most definitely nowhere near a right angle to the track and in that position half the benefit of the shoulder-in movement is lost.

The next most important point to appreciate is that the horse is bent in one continuous curve, in so far as it is possible for a horse to do this, from his croup to his poll. In this connection the most likely fault to occur will be that there will be too much bend in the neck, and when that happens it becomes impossible to obtain or to maintain true impulsion to the hand and the rider loses control. Depending on the extent of the excess bend in the neck, all or most of the impulsion going through the horse will fall out through the shoulder without ever reaching the poll and the mouth. Real impulsion must, in Colonel Hans Handler's words, begin in the quarters, pass through the back and neck and end in the mouth (and therefore in the rider's hand).

Provided we concentrate on and manage strictly to observe the two principles that we have just discussed, that is to say the principle of the quarters and the principle of the single curve, we shall not go seriously wrong in our efforts to perform the movement which must of course be carried out with impulsion. But we must also mention the matter of the degree to which the forehand and forefeet should come inside the track of the quarters and hind feet. This is a matter of technical and almost academic interest that must not be allowed to interfere with the two basic principles of the quarters and the bend. It becomes important in competition dressage where accuracy and consistency are high-scoring qualities, but at all times it should be regarded as of lesser importance than the maintenance of the two basic principles that we have established. Nevertheless, the degree of bend is an interesting matter that we must understand in order to master, and it therefore justifies a detailed discussion.

Degree of bend

A horse moving along a straight line makes two tracks, one with the off-fore and off hind feet and one with the near-fore and near hind. If the forehand is eventually and increasingly taken inwards from the original track while the hind quarters continue along it, first four tracks will be made, then three as the outside forefoot coincides with the track of the inside hind foot, and then again four as both the forefeet make tracks parallel to but inside those of the hind feet. The diagrams in Fig. 7 will make this clear. It will also be clear that there must inevitably be some variation in the relationship of the various tracks under whichever heading they are placed, with the exception that it will always be possible to say whether or not a horse is moving exactly on three tracks in the same way as it is possible to say whether he is exactly straight and moving precisely on two tracks. But for the rider it must always remain a question of guessing since he cannot possibly see exactly where his horse's feet are hitting the ground.

It will also be clear from the diagrams that the greater the bend in the horse from the croup forwards, the further the forefeet will come away from the main track. A very little bend will result in four overlapping tracks; a little more bend and we shall have three tracks which is thought by many, though not by all, to be the classical shoulder-in; and an even greater bend will result in four clearly separated tracks. And each of these three examples, as well as all the intermediate possibilities, can be accurately described as true shoulder-in. So it all depends in the end on what you want to do and how much bend your horse is capable of producing. In other words, and in regard to the latter factor, it depends on the state of training of the horse.

Four-track shoulder-in

To demonstrate the last point, we will consider the method of starting a shoulder-in in which the movement is begun after the completion of a circle and at the exact point at which the circle touches the main track, for example at point E in a manège. If a young horse is only sufficiently supple to be able to bend correctly round the curve of a twenty-metre circle he will not, when we ask him to go shoulder-in at E, be able to show a correct three-track movement. If we make him hold his quarters in the correct position, more or less square with the track as already described, he will just not be able to bend sufficiently to make the three-track possible, and he will show instead four overlapping tracks.

Later, when the horse has become more supple and is able to perform a truly correct ten-metre circle, we can take him off that ten-metre circle at E and, by retaining exactly the same bend as he had on the circle, he will perform a true three-track shoulder-in. But it is still impossible for him to show the movement in four separate tracks unless we are prepared to sacrifice the principle of the quarters by letting them twist out of their square alignment. That of course would help to bring the forehand further in to show four tracks, but it would no longer be a pure shoulder-in and the horse would cease to benefit from the exercise (see Fig. 7c).

A true shoulder-in with four equally spaced tracks will not be possible until the horse is supple enough to be capable of executing a volte of six metres in diameter, and that implies a very advanced standard of dressage. But we are now trying to train a young horse, and it should be clear that all we have to worry about at this stage is that the forehand should come in just a little bit, and that we can safely allow the question of the number and width of tracks to wait for a later stage in our programme.

Purpose of shoulder-in

There are, however, one or two other aspects of the shoulder-in to discuss and clarify before we try to teach it to the horse. We must be clear about its purpose and the result that we hope to obtain from it or else we shall largely be wasting our time. There is nothing special to be gained by just learning to go a little bit sideways on three or four tracks since we have already learned to do it quite nicely on four tracks in leg-yielding. But the shoulder-in, if carried out correctly, has several very special qualities that are important for the rest of the period of training covered in this book and almost indispensable for riders who may wish to give their horses further education into the sphere of advanced dressage. These qualities are so many and so important that it is worth while to set them out separately.

1. The shoulder-in is the easiest, and therefore the first, exercise in going sideways with a bend. We have already learned to go sideways without a bend in leg-yielding, but now we introduce the bend and with it all the gymnastic complications for the horse that we discussed in Chapter 2 in connection with movement with a bend on a circle. It is easier for the horse to learn first to move sideways towards the open or convex side of his body as in a shoulder-in than it is to move towards

the concave or closed side, because all the muscles on that side are freer and less likely to operate in a cramped manner.

2. Provided rhythm and impulsion are maintained, the shoulder-in requires an even looser and more supple action of the shoulders than did the leg-yielding, for the obvious reason that the shoulders are turned at a greater angle from the line of progression than they were in the leg-yielding. A greater degree of crossing is required by the inside foreleg.

3. The shoulder-in is the first exercise deliberately designed to encourage and develop the horse's ability to collect. True, it only has this effect on one hind leg at a time, that is to say on the inner hind leg, but it is no bad thing to deal with one thing at a time and then put two of them together later on. In the trot the collecting effect on the inside hind leg results from two causes. On the one hand the relative freedom of the outside foreleg, on the outside of the bend, encourages the hind leg on the same diagonal to swing further forward under the horse, and in so doing it induces an increased bend in the three joints of that leg. In addition, the fact that the forehand has been brought more or less towards the inside means that the vertical line passing through the horse's centre of gravity, which is just behind the girth, will also have been brought towards the inside, though to a slightly lesser extent than the shoulders and forefeet. It follows that the inner hind foot will, in addition to reaching well forward along its original track, be coming to the ground right under the centre of gravity instead of somewhat to one side of it as is normally the case when the horse is moving straight forward. He thus learns how to begin to carry more of his weight with his hind legs and quarters. By executing the shoulder-in on both reins to a more or less equal extent, the lesson of collection is kept equal.

4. And finally, and perhaps most important of all the lessons of the shoulder-in, is the requirement that the horse should bend round and obey the rider's inside leg applied in a forward direction on the girth. This will develop the invaluable ability of the rider to control his horse, particularly with regard to its straightness, between his inside leg and outside hand.

Aids for shoulder-in

The aids for the shoulder-in will, as in leg-yielding, be predominantly lateral. That is to say, the inside leg predominates by acting on the girth to press the horse's inward bending forehand to the outside along the line of the track. The outside leg is used passively in a withdrawn position to prevent the quarters from falling out or twisting towards the inside. It should also be ready to assist the inside leg with the maintenance of impulsion if necessary. The inside rein acts predominantly with a degree of opposition behind the withers, thus complementing the effect of the inside leg. The outside rein helps to start the movement by leading the horse, with a slight opening effect, into the direction of the track after the forehand has been brought in, but thereafter is confined to supporting the inside rein to control the degree of bend in the neck. Both hands are carried a little to the inside of centre in order to comply with and maintain the bend.

It is very important that the inside leg should be well stretched down from the time that the horse is being prepared for the movement, allowing the rider's weight to fall rather more on to the inside seat bone. This will help to maintain the bend and to push the horse outward towards the convex side. The rider's hips will remain square with the horse's hips, but his shoulders must turn to the inside to follow those of the horse.

If the rider has ridden this movement before, or has been able to practise on a trained horse, the aids should not be difficult for him to apply correctly although perhaps more than in any other movement the shoulder-in stands or falls by the correctness of the rider's aids. If the rider is new to the movement he will be well advised to practise it many times in his imagination in order to get the feel in his own body, especially for the necessary twist in his hips, before trying it with his horse for the first time.

Execution of shoulder-in

So, after refreshing our minds with the theory of the movement as it will affect both horse and rider, we will make a start. And as with many other new lessons we shall begin at the walk. In that pace we shall have less impulsion to control, and horse and rider will both have more time between successive steps to sort out the problems and uncertainties that are bound to arise. We shall try to make the start out of the circle as has already been suggested because that provides us with the most favourable conditions and the best hope of getting it right first time. We want to use the smallest circle that the horse is capable of executing properly at this stage because that will allow us to start the new movement from a more definite shoulder-in position. We will assume that by now we can make a good fifteen-metre circle, but if not then we must make it eighteen or even twenty metres. In any case it must be good with the horse accepting the bend all the way round and taking the outside rein off our inside leg. In particular he must be listening to our inside leg. And because of the radius of the circle we will begin the shoulder-in from any convenient point on the long track of our working area between the quarter marker and the half marker and on the right rein. We will assume that the point of departure on the circle is E (see Fig. 7, p. 116.)

With those essential preliminaries fixed, we proceed along the track in walk and on to the circle to the right at E, remaining in a well-controlled walk, with the horse flexing at the poll.

As we come round to complete the circle we very carefully but deliberately continue on the same curve, as if to begin a second circle, until the line through the horse's two hip bones is precisely opposite E. By that time the horse's forefeet will be about one and a half metres past E and on their way into the new circle. That is the exact moment, not before and not later, when we are positioned correctly in every respect to perform a perfect right shoulder-in. It probably won't turn out to be perfect, but at least we shall have given ourself and the horse the maximum chance. All that remains for us to do is to apply the right aids and obtain the expected response. That may not be quite as easy first time as it sounds, but it will certainly not be very difficult if the preparatory training has been satisfactory.

Our horse has already become conversant with the need to move sideways from leg pressure applied in various places behind the girth during the earlier exercises, and he will probably have no difficulty in understanding how to act when the pressure is felt in a new place considerably further forward and right on the girth. Reacting to that simple logic and to equally simple mechanical effects of the other aids, he will begin to move his forehand to the left. Nothing is being asked of his quarters except that they should not swing outwards, that matter being looked after by our own passive left or outside leg.

Having initially recognized the requirement, the young horse may find the execution a little complicated and strange, and he may become hesitant in his steps and his willingness to keep up to the bit. In that case we can probably help him by gently using the right indirect rein against his neck with a slight lifting effect in time with the lifting and sideways movement of his right or inside foreleg. The movement of that leg is for him both the difficulty and the essence of the shoulder-in, and we should be prepared to help him until he gets used to the action. The lifting action of the hand will quite soon become unnecessary though it can be used again from time to time as and when we feel it would help to freshen the movement.

Once we are confident that he understands the movement we can immediately move forward on to the circle again after each successful effort, so that the horse remains on exactly the same bend as we practise circle, shoulder-in, circle, etc. Naturally, we must never tire or irritate the horse, and there must be frequent breaks on a long rein.

After about a week there should be no doubt about the horse's understanding of the exercise or of his willingness and ability to perform it fairly well and without any fuss at the walk and on both reins. As soon as, but not until, we are confident of that, we can start the same procedure again in the trot. Like the walk, the trot should be an active but steady working pace, and we need expect little trouble of any sort apart from the usual need for patience and help for the young horse to co-ordinate and find his feet in the more finely balanced pace of trot.

All the time, as we improve and can bring this movement more and more freely into our routine, we must remember those two basic principles of the bend and the quarters. We still need not be particularly concerned about the number of tracks that we are making, though if we really want to assuage our curiosity we can invite a friend to come and look and tell us. It is, however, of importance that we should try to obtain the same degree of bend and fluency on both reins, not only because that will please the judges if we ever compete in a test that includes the shoulder-in, but also because it will greatly help us to train the horse with an equal degree of suppleness on both sides.

Straightening the horse

Before we leave the shoulder-in, we must mention one other advantage of this invaluable movement, and that is the ability that it gives the rider in his efforts to straighten a crooked horse. All horses have a greater or lesser tendency to move out of the straight, that is to say that their hind feet do not follow exactly in the tracks of the forefeet. Crookedness involves a severe loss of impulsion in the same way that a coil-spring cannot be put under tension unless it can be kept straight between its two ends. It therefore becomes the trainer's perpetual and prime concern to keep his horse straight and to re-straighten him when he becomes crooked. This is a very difficult task and is often very nearly impossible without the use of the shoulder-in.

Suppose the horse is moving with a hollow right side and is therefore carrying his quarters to the right. If we try to push the quarters back into line with our withdrawn right leg, we shall no doubt succeed in moving the quarters towards the left, but we shall almost certainly have done nothing to cure the unwanted bend of the body to the right. We shall only succeed in putting the horse into a different sort of crookedness that will be even more uncomfortable to sit on than the first. If we try to do that in canter we shall be in even worse trouble because we shall probably cause the horse to change from right lead to left lead or to go disunited. So clearly we have to find a better way.

The shoulder-in gives the rider the ability to place the forehand in front of the errant quarters at any time with both his legs remaining in the position from which they can best maintain impulsion. If we take the same awkward example of the horse cantering right with an excessive right bend and with his quarters falling in to the right, we can deal with the situation by applying with great firmness all the aids for shoulder-in right, not forgetting the weight of the body on the inside seat bone, and then ride for a shoulder-in until we achieve one to a sufficient degree to be fractionally more than straight. This correction is not at all easy to do, but at least it is possible and becomes easier and more effective as both partners get used to it. There is no better way.

There should certainly be no question of our beginning to practise shoulder-in in the canter in its own right at this Phase 4. But it is as well to remember that it will be needed later, and we can be thinking about it now especially if we become conscious that the canter is becoming a little crooked as it is likely to do when we gradually ask for just a little more collection. In fact we cannot think too much about the movement. We must come to live with it as our constant companion and helpmate.

The rein-back

It is time now to teach the rein-back or, if we find that circumstances have forced us to use it already, to teach it now in its correct form. We may well have made a useful start by the simple means of asking the horse to move backwards for a step or two in the stable or outside, for example, just before we mount. We shall have used the vocal aid on such occasions, perhaps reinforced with a touch of the whip on his forearm or knees. If that has happened, so much the better, as we can combine our voice with the other aids when giving the first mounted lesson.

First, we need to remind ourselves of the primary rule that the rider must never pull backwards with the reins. How then do we obtain a rein-back? Well, it is quite easy, as we shall find if only we obey the rules and provided that we know about and understand the mechanical effect of the third or direct rein of opposition. The diagram on page 90 showed its use by one rein only, but if both reins are used simultaneously in the same manner, the combined result can only be to transfer forward impulsion into a backward motion.

The horse is standing still, reasonably square and truly on the bit, with a flexed poll, showing no resistance. We close the legs exactly as if asking him to walk forward. This forward aid is continued until we quite distinctly feel the horse under us begin to sway forward, and at that moment we close the hands firmly on the rein to oppose all further forward movement. But we must not pull, and it will be helpful and will do no harm until we are used to the feel if we press our elbows into our waist so that it is not possible for them or the hands to exert any backward influence. If there is no sign of a rein-back at the first try, relax, move forward to re-establish a good halt and try again. It does and will work, and all we then have to do is to release the pressure of the legs as he begins to oblige us while maintaining the opposition of the hands. Just a few steps will be sufficient at first before we quietly but firmly close the legs again, release the fingers and allow the impulsion to carry us forward into a normal walk. Much later on, in advanced dressage, the rider can play the impulsion back and forth several times, doing nothing but close and open his fingers and legs alternately in a to-and-fro movement called a *schaukel*, which is the German name for a see-saw.

Executed in this manner the horse will almost invariably remain quiet and calm in the steps and free from resistance in the back and mouth. But nature seems to have ensured that horses do not find the rein-back an easy thing, and so we should avoid using it to excess and seldom if ever for more than five or six paces at a time. We should also vary the number of paces we ask for, sometimes insisting on only one, never allowing more than we have predetermined. This helps to avoid any tendency to rush or to anticipate. For a final tip, always give the horse plenty of time to get and take his cue.

Walk to canter

Work in shoulder-in will produce a marked improvement in the horse's responsiveness to the rider's leg aids, and especially to the aid from the inner leg, in all other work and not least for the strike-off into canter. Strike-offs should now be very prompt and, provided that is so, we can begin to work on the strike-off from walk to canter without any intervening steps of trot. This makes considerably more demands on the horse than the canter from trot, as it requires a much more positive jump into the first stride and a more immediate lifting of the weight off the forehand. The big distinction between the speed of the walk and the canter, as compared with the trot and the canter, can only be bridged by a more positive muscular effort of acceleration from the first or outside hind leg. The exercise therefore does a lot to develop muscular strength and carrying power in the quarters and loins as well as the attention and obedience of the horse.

If we are going to ask for a canter-left from the walk, the off hind will be the leg that initiates the canter, followed by the right diagonal, and lastly the left or leading foreleg. In the walk, the off hind will have been followed to the ground by the off-fore, followed by the near hind, and lastly the near-fore. What the horse has to do is to delay slightly the fall of the off-fore and at the same time to speed up the coming forward of the near hind so that those two legs come to the ground together to form the diagonal or second beat of the canter-left. He achieves this by making a little lifting jump from the off hind which results in the off-fore being in suspension a little longer than it would otherwise have been if the walk had been continued. What the rider has to do is to encourage and provoke that little lifting jump, together with the acceleration of the movement of the near hind.

If we think of it in this way, the aids for the strike-off become logical and simple. The lifting jump will be achieved by the seat and leg aids calling for a quick increase in impulsion which will then be sufficiently controlled by the hands so that it tends to go rather more upwards than forwards. In the early stages the horse can be helped and encouraged to produce the lift by a small lifting action of the inside hand to make the message even clearer. But it is only the inside leg that can influence the action of the near hind leg so as to induce the horse to bring it forward more quickly and further underneath so as to coincide with the fall of the off-fore, thus forming the diagonal second beat of the canter-left. It is the formation of that right diagonal that creates the canter, and it is therefore the rider's inside leg that plays the predominant and vital role in the creation of a good strike-off from the walk, or even from the halt or from the trot. The ideal moment to apply the aid will be just as, and certainly not later than, the off hind comes to the ground in the walk, provided the horse has been well prepared and put to the aids in the last strides of the walk. It is that leg that must initiate our canter-left by providing the first thrust forward and upward.

One of the requirements of a strike-off from the walk, and also later on from the halt, is that it should be straight and that there should be no tendency for the horse to move the quarters inwards to facilitate the action of the inside hind leg. That is a natural tendency that has to be counteracted or corrected as it is ugly, implies a loss of control and spoils the impulsion and the power of the movement. But the remedy is to hand and lies in the exercise of the shoulder-in that we have been practising at the same time or perhaps a little earlier than the strike-off. By placing the horse in a very slight shoulder-in position in the preceding walk we have and will be able to keep the forehand well in front of the quarters, and so at least the first stride of the strike-off will contain an element of the same shoulder-in. Here is our first example of the many great benefits of that excellent exercise when applied to other movements of greater importance in themselves. In other words, we can now begin to keep control of the quarters without the direct use of the leg on the side to which the quarters tend to fall.

The strike-off from the walk is essentially a collected movement and will consequently tend to induce some short strides in the canter. So though we can practise it with advantage quite frequently without much risk of overtaxing or upsetting the horse, we should remember to counter-balance the stride-shortening tendency by plenty of free-striding work on a long rein, taking care not to do that too soon after a successful strike-off for fear of exciting the horse by letting him connect the strike-off in his mind with the chance for a good gallop. We should also be careful not to allow the horse to fall on to his forehand during the transition from the short to the longer canter.

The transition from canter to walk is more difficult for the horse and belongs to a later training phase.

Serpentines

Flowing serpentine movements should be introduced and practised in this phase, first in trot and then later also in canter. The important thing in trot serpentines is to be able to change the bend in the horse quite smoothly, consistent with the change on the curve of the chosen serpentine track. To achieve this the rider must be careful and precise in changing his own position and aids in good time and without letting the horse lose balance or rhythm. He must gently keep the impulsion going so as not to lose or even weaken the contact with the bit.

It is best to begin with quite small loops away from and back to the long side of a manège or its equivalent and then later on to do the big serpentines right across the manège. These are best done in rising trot to begin with and without changing the diagonal of the trot. To make it easier for the horse to understand the logic of what he is being asked to do, the rider should clearly over-ride the curves so that they are generously pear-shaped. That way there will be less chance of the horse trying to change direction without changing bend. The more acute the curve of the track, the easier it is for the rider to create and hold the bend in the horse with his inside leg.

Serpentines in canter cannot be started until changes of leg through the walk have been practised, and that will probably not be introduced for several months yet. We can, however, now start changes through the trot on straight lines and then quite soon on very big curves or serpentines if we are working in a field where space is not restricted. But at any rate in the early stages they require too much room in the trot phase to be practical within the confines of a manège or arena, except on the straight lines.

Changes through the trot on straight lines present no great difficulty. They are largely concerned with quick response and obedience from the horse and in teaching him to respond to aids that become increasingly discrete and well co-ordinated. Frequent strike-offs, not always on to the other leg, are excellent for keeping the horse alert, and quite soon we shall possibly be able to achieve our strike-off with little more than a mere shifting of our weight on to the new inside seat bone and stirrup, but always with a slight tendency to a shoulder-in to ensure straightness. We must also watch carefully to see that the downward transitions into the trot go well forward into the hand and that we achieve them through an action very similar to a half-halt that ends with a giving of the hand. There must be no semblance of a check in the first or second stride of the trot, and neither must there be the slightest hesitation into the first stride of the canter. When we can feel proud of our changes through the trot on straight lines or very big curves it will be time to try them on a true serpentine in a manège.

Now that we are at the end of Phase 4 and thus at the end of the first twelve months of our programme, we should consider very seriously the progress that we have made and compare it with the schedule. Primarily, we ought to be confident that the horse is moving freely and supply forward in good balance and with a truly supple back in walk, trot and canter; that if balance is lost it can be regained by the use of a half-halt; that he will remain on the bit in all his work; that he understands elementary lateral work including the shoulder-in; and that he is calm and free from resistance, especially in the poll and jaw. If any of these factors give cause for anxiety, we should quickly seek superior advice and set about remedying the trouble without delay. If all is going according to plan, we can happily launch forth into the even more interesting second year that is dealt with in Part III.

Appendix to Part II

On the forehand

Horses vary enormously in the degree of poise, lightness and agility with which they move of their own accord. These variations are the result of many complicated and subtle differences of physical conformation and also, to some extent, of psychological attitudes. Those less gifted with natural balance and agility will be more difficult to train to an acceptable degree of self-carriage in which their weight is carried more or less equally over all four legs. It will, in common terms, be more difficult to get them off their forehands.

All young horses will be 'on their forehands' to a greater or lesser extent, especially when they have a rider on their back. They will not be able to function effectively until this state of imbalance has been corrected by training processes that require time, skill and patience on the part of the trainer. Moreover, the horse will find it difficult to make the necessary adjustment to his deportment as he gets older and more 'set in his ways', so it becomes dangerous to allow this problem to remain unresolved for too long. The necessary corrections are, of course, a continuous process that has no finality, but the problem should at least be well under control by the end of the first year, at least to the extent that it will not be holding up the normal and expected progress of education. In other words, the horse should be able to perform the movements required in each successive stage of his education from then on without being heavy in hand or heavy on his forelegs.

In theory, the horse will begin to come 'off his forehand' as he gradually develops the strength to carry himself and his rider and, more especially, as he becomes responsive to the half-halts which will have been progressively introduced after the first six months of his training. The horse that is naturally well balanced and has an active character will present no great problem in this respect. But there are certain types of horses, especially those with big heads or heavy fronts, or perhaps with rather weak loins, who will not respond sufficiently and will continue to move with overloaded forehands to the point where their education will be severely hindered. They need some special help. They are by no means necessarily bad horses and certainly need not be 'written off' because of this problem.

The symptoms will usually be felt quite clearly when the horse seemingly drops on to the forehand when turning a corner, performing a downward transition or when doing anything that theoretically ought to be relatively easy and within his compass at any given stage. Preparatory half-halts of the normal kind will have been used conscientiously without effecting substantial improvement, so the rider must look for some other means of producing the result that he must obtain if he is to succeed in his overall objective. It will be of no avail to jab the horse in the mouth with more or less violent rein actions; such a course would be painful and unfair to the horse who would not understand why he was being hurt and would react by throwing up his head and hollowing his back. A hollow-backed horse is always effectively on his forehand, as will be seen from the illustrations on p. 98. The rider must therefore find some means of 'showing' his horse that he has to make a special muscular effort to maintain a more horizontal balance at certain moments and during certain movements, and to encourage him to do it.

This the rider will be able to do by riding his horse – if necessary for quite long periods – just before, during and immediately after the movement which the horse has found difficult, with his hands held much higher than normal. He should take his hands upwards and forwards towards the horse's ears so that the reins will produce a clearly lifting effect without backward pull. Actually, they will not so much lift the horse's head as prevent him from dropping it. He will easily understand where his head is expected to stay and, in his efforts to conform, will inevitably try to carry more of the weight of his forehand with his back muscles.

This method of attacking the problem may seem a little crude at first sight but, as long as the rider is aware that what he is doing is designed to treat an abnormal and temporary problem, he will do no damage. He will accept that the horse's nose will be carried appreciably in front of the vertical while the action is maintained, but the raised hands do not necessitate an uncomfortable position for the horse. They should endeavour to keep up the head rather than the nose.

In difficult cases it may be necessary to use this method of adjusting the horse's carriage on and off for several months. In others, just a few days or a couple of weeks may be sufficient to show marked improvement in the horse's ability to remain in horizontal balance. He will have understood much more clearly just what sort of an effort is being asked of him and will have been positively helped to make that effort and to feel the beneficial results.

Work in the walk

Any rider who starts to train a horse with the intention of taking him through into the higher school of advanced dressage, beyond the scope of this book, will find that there are many benefits to be obtained from the practice of exercising his horse in the collected walk. This form of work can most usefully be introduced, in an increasingly elaborate way, into the daily routine at any time towards the end of the first year of the programme.

This work in the walk involves the use of a quite slow, deliberate but active placing of the four feet in correct sequence in shortened steps. In its simplest form, on straight lines, it makes considerable and even abnormal demands on the mental concentration of the horse as will be appreciated by anyone who himself adopts a similar procedure in walking very slowly along a straight line on the ground. Immediately he will notice that the problems of balance and concentration become more acute and that it is comparatively difficult to co-ordinate the movement of his two legs and two arms. Each limb has to be lifted and advanced in the appropriate direction separately and in a controlled manner, and a conscious effort has to be made to maintain the smooth flow of the overall movement. This exercise is as highly beneficial for the young horse as it is for the human being.

These and other advantages of the work in walk accrue from the fact that it involves no element of hurry or hustle. There is all the time in the world for the rider and the horse to think about the many and subtle problems that they have to overcome at first in order to achieve complete co-ordination of their direct and their reflex actions. There is a very much reduced likelihood of the horse losing balance, and consequently also his rhythm, because he will always retain at least one and often two or three feet on the ground, whereas the trot has frequently recurring moments of total suspension. There will consequently be no need or temptation for the horse to lean on the rider's hand at any time, thus encouraging him at this quite early stage to move in complete self-carriage. Horse and rider together will begin to understand and appreciate the possibilities of lightness and co-operation.

It will very soon be found that the young horse will collect himself without any resistance immediately the rider takes a shortened contact with the reins and asks for collection with a braced back. In these early stages of the exercise the rider's main concern will be to maintain the activity and impulsion of the pace, particularly from the hind legs, without increasing the speed or the tempo which must at all costs remain deliberate and calm. The rider's legs must remain in close and prolonged contact with the horse's sides, enabling him to feel and react with his seat to any deviation of the quarters from the straight line or to any reduction of the activity.

As the horse's suppleness and dexterity improves, it will become possible to introduce some, and eventually all, of the lateral movements with resulting benefit to the harmony, lightness and mutual understanding between horse and rider.

In carrying out this work the horse will learn to come together and to move in one piece to an extent that might take him many more months to achieve by other means. This in turn will greatly improve his ability to achieve and move in a satisfactory collected trot, the latter being one of the most important aspects of the work to be studied in the second year of his training. It will also do a great deal to improve the quality of the walk itself, particularly for those horses that tend to be somewhat one-paced in walk and have difficulty in making the variations between a free or extended stride and the medium or more collected version of the pace.

The normal variations of the walk should naturally be practised regularly so that they are not neglected, but the work in collected walk as here described can increasingly take its place as a major aspect of routine training. Not the least of its advantages will be the use that can be made of it when exercising a horse on land that is too wet for useful work in trot or canter. A very constructive half-hour can be spent, and be sufficient for the animal's minimum needs, when it is virtually impossible to use the faster paces.

PART III

Practical Work: The Second Year

Improving collection. The author on Burak.

CHAPTER TEN

Entering the Second Year
Phase 5 (Months 13–15)

Travers. 15 metre canter circles. Collection. Medium trot.
Canter changes. Straightening. 10 metre trot circles. 8 metre trot
half circles. More impulsion. More half-halts. Turn on the haunches.

The entry into the second year of the training programme justifies
something rather more than the normal three-monthly check. It is a
milestone that marks the beginning of the most important year in the
young horse's life, the point perhaps at which he must cease to be regarded as a baby and be required now to work really hard. Naturally, we
shall not suddenly change our methods and attitudes overnight and the
increase in work pressure will in practice be very gradual, but at least
we should now feel quite confident in pressing on with the rather more
demanding exercises in the forthcoming schedules with the knowledge
that our horse has had plenty of time to find his feet and will now be
physically and mentally able to tackle virtually anything that we may
ask of him. But since this book is intended to help the less experienced
rider, we shall continue to make progress at a controlled rate.

Collection

The idea of collection will have been in our mind from the earliest stages
of our training programme, though hitherto it will have taken second
place in favour of free, forward movement and suppleness, in that order.
From now on, however, collection must, albeit in a tactful way, take
pride of place in our list of priorities. But we cannot approach it in a
hurry; rather it must be introduced into the system through the suppleness and as a special quality of the free, forward movement.

A horse that is not collected is uncollected, and an uncollected horse is one that tends more or less to sprawl in his paces. He will not be able to marshal and control his forces to their best advantage and will consequently not be in a position to respond easily and quickly to the demands of his rider. The good riding horse must therefore be able to work with a clear and substantial degree of collection.

True and useful collection has to be obtained without spoiling the suppleness that we have been at such pains to instil. Therefore, we must never try to obtain it by pulling back the front of the horse by the reins, which would perhaps be the most instinctive approach of most inexperienced riders. We have rather to teach the horse to collect himself, from the back to the front, and we do this by asking for more activity and impulsion from the quarters while containing the speed with the reins. With the forehand thus remaining free and unrestricted, the horse will, provided his back and spine remain supple, tend to catch up with himself from the back forwards, and to do that he will tend, just a little, to bend the joints of his hind legs so that they can reach that little bit further under his mass. That will cause the quarters to lower, just a little, in relation to the forehand; they will carry a little more of the overall weight, and the horse will become that little bit lighter in hand and more easily able to control his forces.

The theory of collection as set out in the preceding paragraph is logical enough and not too difficult to understand, but it is a good deal more difficult to practise, and progress cannot be expected to be other than slow. For example, its development has to wait upon the development of the appropriate and necessary muscles in the back, neck, loins and quarters that alone make it possible for the horse to begin to carry additional weight on the quarters. The development of those muscles, and their sequel, must therefore lie at the heart of all gymnastic training from its very earliest stage. If that development, in the right manner and for the right purpose, is delayed too long there will come a time when it may be too late. Collection, by means of the shoulder-in, the half-halts, lateral work and overall suppleness, must be worked on from the beginning but with tact, understanding and patience. Gradually it has to be incorporated into all the work including the extensions.

Medium trot

We should by now have begun to develop the medium trot. The working paces – that is to say the type of pace or gait that, though active, is sufficiently controlled for the horse to be able to maintain it indefinitely without excessive strain – will have been fully established, but we must guard against the danger of the horse becoming one-paced and inflexible. So we must introduce a greater variety in the length of stride in order to stretch his muscles and generally increase his gymnastic ability.

The medium pace, whether it be walk, trot or canter, must contain a distinctly recognizable element of extension emanating from an increased impulsion as compared with the much more easy-going working pace, but it should by no means verge on the true extended pace. In trot and canter the medium pace will require a considerably more determined jump and thrust from the hind legs that will quickly tire the horse at first, and indeed it will always make any horse feel the strain if kept up for more than a few hundred metres at most. That can be compared with the fifty to sixty metres that is more than enough for a fit and well-trained horse in full extension in trot.

There are two dangerous pitfalls that we have to avoid when teaching the medium trot. The first concerns the fact that, if we demand too much at the outset, the horse will tend to come off the bit by poking his nose and stiffening his back in his honest endeavours to achieve the degree of extension that is being asked of him. This can easily become a habit that will be difficult to cure and will spoil all extended work as well as making him uncomfortable to sit on. The mouth and the back will both become hard and unmanageable. We must therefore ask for the transition into medium trot only when we are sure that the horse is soft, round, free of resistance in the back, and nicely on the bit. It is vital that the rider also remains supple in his back and legs while making the demand. We must then be careful to ask for the increased impulsion and length of stride only to the extent that he can respond without losing those qualities, and we must cease the demanding aids of leg and back immediately we feel we are losing the softness. It is an illusion to think that we shall be able to regain the lost softness once the horse is in full but stiff action, so we must just never let that occur, and it requires no little strength of will to restrain our own urge to get some sort of extension at all or any cost.

The other pitfall concerns the probable tendency of the horse to respond to our aids by quickening the tempo instead of lengthening the stride. This frequently occurs and is quite difficult to counteract. In fact, the only true remedy is to improve the rhythm of the working trot, if possible to the extent of obtaining a degree of cadence in it, before asking once more for a very little lengthening into a medium pace. Over and over again it will be found that, when the working trot is really good, there will be no difficulty in obtaining a satisfactory medium trot. It will come with hardly any effort at all.

In addition to those two major problems, we may find that the horse tends to lose balance and go on his forehand in the more extended paces. He will reach out with his forelegs, but he will find it less easy to complement that action with an increased forward reach of the hind legs which will consequently be carrying less weight. Any tendency to fall on to the forehand in this manner must be quietly but clearly corrected by restarting the movement and by taking extra trouble to ensure that the horse is really well balanced at the beginning and retains the balance in the first three or four strides of the new pace. The movement must be discontinued as soon as the horse ceases to be able to carry himself in a horizontal posture. We must be content with a little of what we want at first, and only ask for more when we feel confident of getting it without loss of quality.

The medium trot can be practised at this stage either on straight lines or on large circles, the latter having the advantage of making it easier to retain suppleness because the curvature of the figure and of the horse inhibits stiffness and resistance. In either case, frequent transitions into and out of the medium pace are an excellent form of gymnastic exercise for the development of the horse's musculature, balance, impulsion and general responsiveness.

The aids for a medium trot should in the end amount to little more than a lengthening and closing of the legs well forward on the girth, accompanied by a bracing of the back, an opening of the shoulders and a very slight giving of the fingers to make it possible for the horse to lengthen his neck and slightly open the angle of the poll. It is very important the rider should not allow the opening of his shoulders to result in his leaning back behind the vertical; this would tend to stiffen the horse's back and make it more difficult for the rider to follow the energetic forward movement with an increase in the movement in the small of his own back. By the same token he must not lean forward as this would reduce the driving influence of his seat. And once more we must remember that the dialogue between the hands and the mouth must be lively enough before and during the transition to ensure that the horse remains flexed at the poll throughout the whole process and consequently retains the ability to swing his back. This latter factor of the hand/mouth dialogue is equally important when it comes to the downward transition from the medium to working trot. Here again the hands must not be allowed to drop on to the withers or become stiff and un-communicative. They have a big part to play in the all too frequent problem of retaining the suppleness of the horse's poll and back in any downward transition.

Further work on half-halts

Without half-halts we shall not make satisfactory progress towards collection, which is going to be a matter of prime importance from now on. They should be practised daily in a firm and clear but simple manner in the trot and on both reins. The horse must be brought back to walk and then immediately released into the trot once more, and the lesson repeated many times until the reaction is such that the horse can be felt to be giving the whole of himself to the task and virtually making the transitions of his own accord as soon as he feels the signal coming through to him. We also regularly practise the same exercise for canter to trot and back to canter. He will learn to carry himself without any reliance on the rider's hand and will become lighter and more supple as a result of the repeated efforts.

Suppose we have walked our horse on a loose rein for a few minutes after leaving the stable. And suppose we have then stretched and loosened him in trot, or in canter if he finds that pace easier, with a long, low neck and a fairly long rein and long strides. He is warm and men-tally ready to begin work. We now take him on to a large circle in a working or lightly collected trot – lightly but fully on the bit with a true flexion in the poll. When we are sure that the horse is free from resistance we make a transition to walk by means of the correct half-halt aids that have already been described and immediately revert to the same collected trot. We repeat the same transition down to walk and up again to trot several times, trying each time to ensure that the horse never comes off or above the bit and does not even try to do so. Some horses, when they are well trained, may give the rider the feel he wants almost at once, though not all horses will do this and it cannot be expected of young animals. There is almost certain to be a degree of resistance somewhere between the back and the mouth to begin with, and the downward transition will consequently be prolonged, as also will be the subsequent upward transition to trot. But there should be an improvement in softness and submission each time the exercise is repeated until eventually the horse accepts and absorbs the demand for the downward transition by giving perceptibly in the poll.

He must show a true walk and then go back into trot, when asked, with the same freedom from any resistance or loss of balance, just lengthening a little as we release the fingers slightly and invite him to trot. The horse must, in short, give in to the rider and signify his readiness to obey rein and leg aids with total submission, however long that takes. In effect this will also bring about a very definite quickening of the horse's responsiveness to all the aids, and particularly to the leg aids. The time spent in the walk between the trots should be reduced until it only just exists.

Once the rider is satisfied with the trot–walk–trot transitions, he should repeat the same thing with canter–trot–canter, and again he will continue until the transitions are obtained softly, supply and on the bit both into and out of the slower pace. Again it may take two or three minutes, five or six minutes, or ten minutes to achieve a satisfactory state of communication, but there must be no giving in except by the horse. No roughness will be needed, just patience, determination and perception by the rider. The desired result will surely come and then, but not till then, the horse will be in a fit mental and physical state to be ridden with mutual co-operation through all the exercises in which he has been or is being trained.

We have been talking about transitions, but in effect we have been talking about the practice of the basic form of the half-halt in its simplest form. With each double transition we have braced, restrained and re-established the original pace. But in doing so we have allowed the horse ample time to understand and comply with each of the three stages. By introducing in each case a slower gait we have minimized the likelihood of any misunderstanding about exactly what we are asking him to do.

Once he has, at the beginning of each day's work, shown himself ready and able to perform and absorb a series of half-halts in what we might call slow motion, we can reasonably expect him to co-operate with the very much more subtle and varied forms in which we wish to employ half-halts while carrying out all the work in the training reper-toire. It might be a straightforward form such as would be required to bring a horse down from a medium to a collected trot, or it might be of a type that would be virtually invisible to a spectator but used to prepare a horse for a flying change in canter or any other exercise that requires the maximum quality of balance. The variety of half-halts, as well as the reasons for using them, are infinite, and their full benefits will only be acquired by practice and experience, but they are all more or less sophisticated modifications of the basic form that has been described in the preceding paragraphs. Both rider and horse must master that first before learning to develop and refine it.

Improving impulsion

Considerable space has been devoted to explaining the whole subject of half-halts because they are vital to the training processes, but at the same time they embody a technique that is somewhat in advance of what is usually understood and practised by most run-of-the-mill riders. Much thought and study is required if the full subtleties are to be mastered. The results will amply repay the effort.

The check and drive-on effect of half-halts is bound to result in an improvement in the quality of impulsion. The mere fact that they help to eliminate resistance will allow the impulsion to be both softer and at the same time fuller and more genuine. When that sort of balance and impulsion can be combined with the collection that we began working on in the previous phase through the practice of the shoulder-in move-ment, we shall begin to feel the sense of controlled power that is the ultimate joy of riding a supple, trained horse. It can indeed be said that the shoulder-in and the half-halt together form the foundation of all training, and both must be practised and polished assiduously if high-quality results are desired.

It is often misleadingly suggested that collection, which implies the engagement of the hind legs further under the horse, can always be achieved if the rider uses his seat and legs sufficiently strongly. But this is to over-simplify and even to misunderstand the nature and the mechanics of the problem, the fact being that no horse can further engage his hind legs unless his poll, neck and back – his whole spine, in fact – is supple and free from resistance. That condition by no means always exists with most horses, but with the shoulder-in and the half-halt at our disposal we have two highly effective means of bringing it about. We must not try or expect to achieve too much collection too soon, but we must work for it steadily, little by little, in keeping with the degree of longitudinal suppleness attained by the horse and con-sequently with his ability to absorb the action of the half-halts right through the body from the poll to the hind legs. In doing this we should be careful not to ask for collection in a dull, persistent way, but should always employ a frequent interchange of pace, alternating the collected, the working and the medium trot or canter. By doing this we shall avoid overstraining the horse's muscles and losing their freshness and resilience. We shall also remain more aware of the degree of success we are achieving and be better able to appreciate the quality of the collection when it is given us.

We also have to remember that the more often collection is asked for the greater becomes the tendency for the horse to become crooked as a natural means of avoiding the stresses involved in collection. But collection can only be effective and useful if and when the quarters are moving in the correct alignment under perfect control. Consequently, we have to be constantly on guard against this crooked tendency which will increase and become more difficult to cure if it is not checked. Fortunately the means to do this now lie to hand in the shoulder-in. Whenever we feel or even anticipate that the quarters are moving out of true alignment we must counteract that by moving the forehand into a shoulder-in position so as to impose it in front of the quarters. The degree of shoulder-in will probably only need to be very slight and indeed cannot be otherwise where the canter is concerned. At times it may only be necessary to indicate shoulder-in by sitting in a shoulder-in position in the saddle. At other times it may be necessary to apply the full shoulder-in aids quite strongly. It depends on the degree of crookedness and the type of movement being carried out. But whatever the degree, the thought should never be far from our minds if we want to have a straight horse under us during his education on the flat.

Travers

Fairly early in this fifth phase of the training programme we should be ready to introduce the next step in lateral work which, after the shoulder-in, will be the travers. This movement is also called the 'head to the wall' or 'quarters-in', but the single word travers is preferred, especially for those riders who operate in wide open spaces. The travers has its counterpart in the very similar movement called renvers, though the distinction between the two is only recognizable when they are executed within a clearly defined arena or manège.

A correct travers, which is illustrated opposite, can be regarded as a sort of first cousin to the shoulder-in. In the latter, it will be remembered, the forehand is required to move parallel to but not on the main track on which the quarters remain straight and square. In the travers, it is the forehand that remains straight, or nearly straight, on the main track while the quarters move along a parallel track. In both movements the horse must be continuously bent from poll to croup. In the shoulder-in

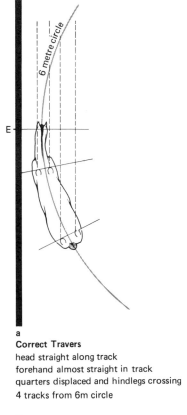
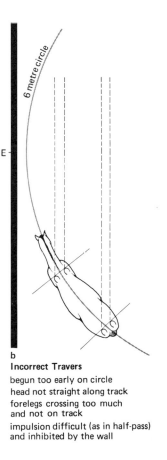

a
Correct Travers
head straight along track
forehand almost straight in track
quarters displaced and hindlegs crossing
4 tracks from 6m circle

b
Incorrect Travers
begun too early on circle
head not straight along track
forelegs crossing too much
and not on track
impulsion difficult (as in half-pass)
and inhibited by the wall

Figure 8

he is bent away from the direction of movement, in the travers he is bent towards the direction of the movement. Both movements can be most easily performed correctly from a circle and from the exact point where that circle touches the straight track. The shoulder-in begins at the precise moment when the quarters reach the touch-point on the circle, the forehand having already passed it. The travers begins at the precise moment when the shoulders reach the touch-point on the circle, the quarters not yet having reached the track. The degree of curve or bend in the horse, and therefore the overall width of the tracks, will be dictated by the size of the circle that the horse is able to execute correctly, and should therefore be the same in both movements.

The travers should not be confused with, or thought to be the same as, the half pass, and the rider should be clearly aware of the differences which are several and important. They are:

1.   In travers, the forelegs move more or less straight and do not cross each other. In half pass, both fore and hind legs cross each other to an equal extent and move at the same angle to the alignment of the horse's body.

2.   In travers the horse is bent consistently and as strongly as his training permits from poll to croup. In half pass, he is almost straight in the body and only slightly bent in the neck. In fact, the half pass is more akin to leg-yielding except that the neck is bent and the poll flexed in the direction of the movement.

3.   In travers the flow of impulsion and the alignment of the forehand remain identical. In the half pass a large part of the impulsion, plus the direction of movement, are required to flow on a different alignment to the body and, in particular, to the forehand of the horse. For this reason alone the half pass is the more complicated and difficult movement of the two, requiring great care in ensuring that not too much forward impulsion is lost so that the horse in effect comes off the bit.

4.   The travers is basically, just like shoulder-in and for the same reasons, a movement on three tracks, though it may come on to four tracks when the horse becomes more supple. The half pass is essentially and always fully four-tracked with a substantial gap between the twin tracks of the forelegs and those of the hind legs. It can never be on three tracks.

5.   The purpose of the travers, or its usefulness, is more closely connected with leg-yielding than with half passing, in that it has practically no collecting effect. The travers asks for a bend throughout the body which leg-yielding does not, and is therefore a suppling exercise for the body. But mainly it is concerned with causing the hind legs to move on a different track and in a different manner from the forelegs, thereby loosening and suppling the whole of the hind quarters while having very limited effect on the forehand. The half pass, on the other hand, exerts a precisely equal effect as regards those two qualities on the quarters and on the forehand.

The correct performance of the travers requires that the rider shall be able to keep the forehand virtually straight on the chosen track while causing the quarters to change their relative position and move along a parallel track. The control of the forehand is done by the rider's inside leg acting well forward on the girth, as in shoulder-in. The positioning and control of the hind legs is done by the positive use of the rider's outside leg drawn back about a hand's-breadth behind the girth, the toe being kept pointing well to the front so that the flat of the upper and lower leg is used rather than the heel. Both hands are carried a little to the inside to comply with the bend, the predominant rein being the outside one acting in close conjunction with the inside leg. The weight of the body should be central, with the rider's outside shoulder being brought well forward. Impulsion must be maintained by the active use of both legs, notwithstanding the fact that they both have their own special part to play in the movement as already described.

The travers, like the shoulder-in, can usefully be introduced on the circle as well as on straight lines. When used on the circle it increases the suppling effect on the forehand and shoulders because they will then be moving on a larger circle than the hind legs, and will consequently have to cover more ground with each stride while the hind legs take correspondingly shorter strides. In order to make even greater demands on the horse's powers of co-ordination and obedience, we can cause him to interchange directly from the shoulder-in (forelegs crossing, hind legs not crossing) to the travers (hind legs crossing, forelegs not crossing) and back again, and this can be done on straight lines or on the circle. This interchanging exercise is also highly beneficial to the rider's own powers of co-ordination and feel.

It is advisable, after every period of work in travers, however short, that the rider should give a very precise and clear indication with his inside leg re-positioned just behind the girth that the quarters must be re-positioned directly behind the forehand and that the travers exercise has been terminated. By that means the horse will learn that a deviation of the quarters will not be tolerated except when specifically asked for.

Turn on the haunches

It will become apparent by now that we have gradually developed and established a fairly comprehensive system of communication and control of the horse through the various positions and pressures of the rider's legs. Gradually, the horse is becoming more and more attentive and quick in his reactions when we make some fairly subtle change of position or pressure. From the somewhat primitive turn on the forehand through leg-yielding, shoulder-in and travers, he is becoming accomplished in his ability and willingness to move part or all of his body away from the direction in which he is facing. It is therefore now time to introduce him to the turn on the haunches, or half pirouette in walk, as it is more conventionally called. This is in effect a form of lateral movement that

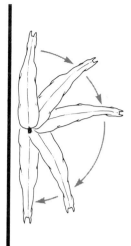

Figure 9 *Half turn on the haunches*

looks much easier than it is in reality if it is to be done correctly. That is the reason why it is best to postpone until this stage an apparently quite simple movement.

The turn on the haunches in walk requires the forehand to move around on a half circle, or part of a circle, with a radius exactly equivalent to the length of the horse while the hind legs continue to function in correct walk sequence without making any ground. They walk virtually on the spot, or on a tiny circle the size of a plate. Usually there will be no great difficulty in moving the forehand round the outer circle in at least a reasonably calm and correct manner, though it may take some time before it can be accomplished with a consistently correct bend in the direction of the movement while remaining on the bit with well-maintained impulsion. But the difficulty arises when the rider has to check the horse's natural tendency to turn on his centre. The quarters must not be allowed to swing outwards in the smallest degree, and at the same time they must actively maintain the proper sequence of the footfall of the walk. The latter point in particular requires a degree of readily obtainable impulsion and collection that will not be available to the rider in the earlier stages of training as when, for example, the turn on the forehand was taught.

It has already been suggested that one of the chief aims of all horsemanship is the better control of the horse's quarters, and that one of the most effective means of achieving that aim is the use of lateral work. The turn on the haunches is a refined form of lateral work on the smallest possible circle and as such should only be attempted when we are satisfied that the horse is ready for it, having mastered the less difficult lateral forms. There are some arguments in favour of postponing the passade and the turn on the haunches until after the half pass, introduced in Phase 6.

In theory at any rate the aids for the turn on the haunches are straight-forward enough. Preceded by a half-halt to shorten the strides of the walk as much as possible, the forehand is led round, say, to the right, by the opening right rein which also requests and maintains the right flexion. It is supported by the left rein against the horse's neck, so that both hands are carried a little to the right. The left rein also opposes undue forward movement and prevents overmuch bend. The rider's left leg ensures that the quarters do not deviate to the left, which would result in a turn on the centre. The left leg also has to support the right leg in maintaining impulsion to keep the horse up to the bit. The right leg controls the speed of the turn.

In practice there is plenty to do to co-ordinate these actions according to the requirements created by the imperfections of the horse's reactions. Perhaps the most important and practically effective thing to remember is to ensure that the outside, in this case the left, seat bone carries a very full share of the rider's weight from the very moment that the turn is asked for. The weighting of the outside seat bone will act powerfully to control the correct turning of the quarters by pushing towards the direction of the turn, and will also enable the rider to feel instantly any tendency or inclination of the horse to stop walking or to resist the correct turn. Forewarned in that way, the rider will be able to take timely corrective or preventive action with more powerful leg aids.

The passade

In view of the almost universal problem of keeping the hind legs active in walk sequence throughout the turn, it is advisable to begin by teaching the passade and not to attempt the true turn on the haunches until the passade, an easier movement, has been thoroughly mastered. The passade, as will be seen in the illustration, is a form of elongated turn on two tracks, its great advantage in this context being that the hind legs have to remain active in the sequence of the selected gait, in this case the walk, in order to make the necessary ground to the side while the turn progresses. The horse begins the movement as a half pass on a small half circle which is then drawn out to a point on the original track, some three or four metres behind the point at which the passade began.

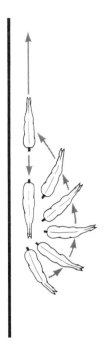

Figure 10   *The Passade*

The horse remains on two tracks until the precise moment when he regains the track when, if the movement has been performed correctly, he will again be straight on one track, having covered more ground with the front legs than with the hind legs. But the value of the passade lies in the fact that the hind legs do have to keep moving.

We do not need to worry unduly at this stage about whether or not the correct bend in the direction of the movement is being maintained. It can equally well be done for training purposes with the horse virtually straight as in leg-yielding. The correct bend can be introduced later when the horse has learned to handle the basic movement with a certain degree of dexterity. It can also be noted here that the passade can also be executed in trot and canter but is much more difficult at those paces and belongs to a phase of training beyond that which is covered in this book.

As the horse's dexterity and understanding of the passade becomes fairly well established, so the size of the movement can be gradually reduced until, almost without noticing it and without any special effort, we shall be making a correct if slightly big half pirouette. But even then the passade should continue to be practised frequently, interspersed with the half pirouette, to ensure that the rider does not lose the ability to keep the hind legs diligently working in the proper walk sequence. The frequent use of the passade helps to create and then to maintain that habit.

Changes from canter to walk

If the half-halts have been assiduously practised during the previous two phases so that we can now feel the control work smoothly and easily through the whole horse without meeting any resistance, we ought to be using them in the form of downward transitions not only from canter to trot but also directly to walk. The latter is a fairly difficult but important lesson as it provides a clear indication of the quality of the balance that we have achieved in the canter. When the horse and rider are in full control of the canter, it will be possible to make a canter–walk transition without any intervening steps of trot. The change of gait can then be clear-cut and effortless. This may take a considerable time to perfect, but the result will be invaluable when we come to work, as we shall do in a few months' time, on the flying change in canter.

Circles

Apart from these major innovations and the usual recapitulations, our daily time schedule during this fifth phase can be fully occupied by improving the work on circles. Particular reference should be made to the quality of the rhythm of the pace and the correctness of the bend as the circles are gradually reduced in size, thus putting lateral suppleness at a premium. If we try to force the horse to make circles that are too small for his state of suppleness and balance we shall end up with broken or unlevel paces and probably also with a tendency for the horse to swing his quarters either in or out which, if it becomes a habit, can be quite difficult to cure. Nevertheless, provided the rider is aware of these dangers and works with due caution, he should make steady progress, and can safely aim by the end of this phase to be performing satisfactory trot circles down to ten metres, canter circles down to fifteen metres and, if everything is going well, he can be trying trot half circles down to eight metres thereby looking ahead two phases when he will want to complete full circles of that size. And as he begins to think about eight-metre circles he should remember that the classic volte is six metres and that that is normally expected only of advanced dressage horses. For those with more modest horizons, a good eight-metre circle is something to be proud of and is not all that easy.

CHAPTER ELEVEN

Developing Lateral Work
Phase 6 (Months 16–18)

*Renvers. Counter canter. Trot half pass. Medium canter.
Laterals on circles. Simple changes. More half-halts. Collected canter.
8 metre trot circles.*

As usual we have to strive constantly to improve and polish the reper-
toire that we have studied to date, and in that connection we must be
humble enough to accept the fact that it is not only the horse that requires improvement. Every rider will learn a little each time he works on
a horse, and every rider is also liable to slip unknowingly into bad habits
and bad postures unless he is frequently checked by someone else or by
his own active sense of self-criticism. It is impossible to overestimate the
influence, for good or for bad, of the rider's seat and the way he uses his
aids on the performance of his horse and, more particularly, of a young
horse in course of training. It is literally true to say that only the very
best seat, posture and aids will produce good work from the horse. Bad
or poor riding will inevitably produce bad or poor results. It follows
that though the rider is ostensibly training the horse, he has first and all
the time to train himself. And when some movement from the horse
seems to fall short of what was expected, the rider should immediately
reflect that 'if the pupil hasn't learnt, the teacher hasn't taught', and act
accordingly by putting his own performance under the microscope.

Half pass

It is time now to make a start on one of the most interesting, useful and
pleasurable lessons in the normal training of any riding horse. This is
the half pass, which is performed in all three basic gaits. The half pass
can also be very frustrating because of the ease with which the horse can

An impeccable half pass by Nuno Oliveira.

contrive to do it badly. In this phase we shall begin in the lesson at the walk, as with all other lateral movements, and then progress after perhaps a few days to the half pass in trot. The canter will not be attempted till the next three-monthly phase, partly because many young horses tend to become excited by the half pass in that pace, and partly because it is as well to allow plenty of time to get the movement freely accepted and well performed in the easier paces of walk and trot.

The half pass involves moving along a line running diagonally to the original line of advance (see diagrams), the horse remaining aligned on that original line. To make a half pass to the right from the centre line of an arena the horse has to cross his left front and hind legs over and in front of his right front and hind legs so as to move diagonally to the right while remaining parallel to the centre line. The half pass is therefore very similar to leg-yielding, which the horse has already learned, but with the added sophistication that he must at the same time be slightly bent and looking in the direction of the movement. However, the classic requirements of the half pass call for the greater part of the bend to be shown in the neck, the body remaining almost straight.

The preparation for the half pass has already been carried out in teaching leg-yielding and the shoulder-in. In both exercises the horse has learned to move away from the leg wherever it is applied, and in the latter he has learned to bend around and to accept the controlling influence of the inside leg applied on the girth. From those lessons we have all we need to create a half pass and to control it. We must, however, remember that this will be the first exercise in which the horse is asked to respond to diagonal, as opposed to lateral aids. That is the chief

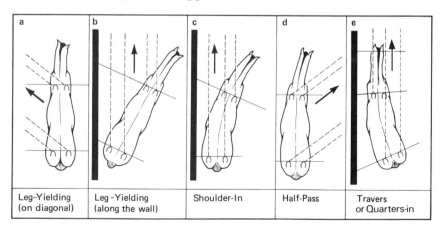

a	b	c	d	e
Leg-Yielding (on diagonal)	Leg-Yielding (along the wall)	Shoulder-In	Half-Pass	Travers or Quarters-in

Figure 11 *Basic lateral movements*

sophistication and therein lies one of the chief values of the half pass, diagonal aids giving the rider far more control of his horse than the somewhat open-ended lateral ones.

We should by now have developed the shoulder-in to the stage where we can obtain it without any difficulty at any time and in any place at the walk or at the trot. On the day that we decide to ask for a half pass for the first time, we initially polish up the shoulder-in in the walk and we choose a spot in the working area where there is a long straight line, hedge or fence that we can regard as the wall of an arena, assuming no proper arena exists. We walk the horse in a well-controlled manner along the fence several times and in both directions so that he comes to regard it, if he has not already done so, as his home ground. Then, as we approach one end of the track along the fence, we make a fairly small half circle away from the fence, say to the right, and immediately, making use of the bend obtained in the half circle, ask for a right shoulder-in as we move down the straight line parallel to the original track by the hedge.

Now, immediately the shoulder-in is established, or after only one or two paces, we shift our weight off the inside seat bone so that we are sitting with our weight central; we release most of the pressure from our inside leg that was creating the lateral movement to the left in the shoulder-in; and we press firmly inwards with the whole of the outside or left leg, from the seat bone downwards, in the same position that it was already in for the shoulder-in, that is to say a little behind the girth. Our hands remain in the same position as they were, slightly to the right of centre, but the inside rein must now lead to the right instead of opposing as was its job in the shoulder-in. The outside rein must allow less bend than before and must, if necessary, apply a degree of opposition in order to assist the outside leg in causing the quarters to move on to their own separate track, parallel to the track of the forelegs. This is a half pass.

What we have done is to make use of the fact that the position of the horse in right shoulder-in is almost exactly the same as the correct position, *vis-à-vis* his alignment, for the right half pass. Almost exactly, but not quite, because there will probably have been a little more bend throughout the horse in the shoulder-in than we need for the half pass where the movement becomes more difficult as the bend increases. So it becomes merely a matter of which of the rider's legs is dominant and whether he is sitting to the inside, as in shoulder-in, or central as in half pass. As a result of his previous lessons the horse will have no difficulty in understanding and responding to the dominant pressure of the inside leg (shoulder-in) or to that of the outside leg (half pass). The slight changes in the rider's weight adjustment and in the rein effects as described in the previous paragraph are largely mechanical and will require little thought on his behalf.

By making a fairly small half circle off the original track by the fence we shall have begun the half pass from a point only a few metres away from that track, and this will help us because the young horse will have a natural and quite noticeable inclination to drift back to the fenced track on which he feels more confident and at home than when working on open and unmarked areas. When we first ask for the half pass there may be a moment of doubt in which he will question the strange movement that appears to be asked of him. But calm, firm persistence of the correct aids, without any resort to whip or spur, will almost invariably produce a few distinct steps of the movement, and in those few steps he will find himself arriving back on the main track where he will be urged to walk forward with a pat on the neck as if nothing strange had happened.

Half pass in trot

We can now repeat the lesson several times on the same rein and then again on the other rein, but only in a quiet though collected walk. After a day or two at most we should be able to do the same exercise in trot, still using the homing instinct of the horse towards the main track to help the smooth flow of the movement. Quite soon we shall be able to ask for short half passes in trot or walk at greater distances from the track or from the track itself towards the centre line or the open spaces of the working area in a field. We must beware of the temptation to continue the half pass lesson for too long a period or for too long a distance at first as it is much more tiring for the horse to move sideways into the bend than to do any form of leg-yielding.

There are a number of points that it is important to remember in work in half pass, and it will be as well to list them in some detail for ease of checking from time to time. We shall undoubtedly be doing a lot of this work, and we must be sure that we always give the horse the best possible chance of doing the movement correctly.

1.   We must always ensure that any half pass starts with the horse looking in the direction in which he is to go and with the forehand slightly

in advance of the quarters. That position must be established before the horse is asked to take the first step sideways. The shoulder-in position is ideal for the purpose.

2. The rider should start with and maintain a slight opening effect with the inside rein which must never be pulled or pressed back across the withers, as that would inhibit the freedom of the shoulders that we particularly wish to encourage. The best way to ensure the opening effect is to turn the thumb outwards so that the palm of the hand becomes more or less visible. That slight movement of the hand is sufficient to indicate to the horse that he is to change direction.

3. The rider's outside shoulder must not be allowed to drop back in the effort to make the quarters move sideways, as that again would inhibit the horse's shoulders. Nevertheless, the contact of the outside rein must be well maintained, the rein pressing lightly against the horse's neck.

4. The rider must, like the horse, look in the direction in which he wants to go and should lean slightly in that direction but without taking weight off the outside seat bone.

5. The rider must resist the temptation to draw the outside leg too far back or to turn the toe out so as to use the back of his boot instead of the whole length of the flat, inside part of his leg. The latter is much more effective in moving the whole horse, and only in that position is it able to assist the inside leg in maintaining impulsion.

6. The more impulsion the rider can maintain in the hand, the easier he will find it to achieve a flowing sideways movement. Impulsion must therefore be his prime concern, not hurrying or rushing forward, but with the horse well up to the bit and asking for directions.

7. If the movements begin to falter in any way, the cure lies not in struggling on with a bad job but in re-establishing the straight forward movement or even going back to the shoulder-in and then restarting the half pass. The ability to alternate the half pass with the shoulder-in as a means of controlling or correcting the half pass demonstrates yet again the recurrent importance of keeping the horse responsive to the controlling effect of the inside leg aid on the girth.

If we find that the horse tends to stiffen and therefore to resist the half pass, it will be a mistake to try to force him into the movement as that would assuredly increase his apprehension. We must, on the contrary, devise means of getting him to accept the half pass aids in a relaxed manner and to learn that it is quite an easy movement if he allows it to be. To this end we have several things to try. We should almost certainly revert for a day or two to leg-yielding, as there is no better way of destroying stiffness. We can try asking for the half pass in rising trot in order to be doubly sure that we are not causing any discomfort to the horse's back by being, perhaps, a little stiff in our own. And we can take more care to ensure that the preliminary shoulder-in steps are correct and supple.

To find the best corrective exercise will largely be a matter of trial and error and of making an intelligent study of the particular type of resistance being encountered. It is impossible to lay down a general rule beyond saying once more that we must not try to force through an already bad half pass.

On the other hand, as soon as we obtain some steps that are fluent and free from resistance, we must remember to pat the horse's neck immediately and then ride forward, probably in rising trot, to make it clear that we are releasing him from a job well done.

Renvers

In addition to the half pass, we can now practise the renvers, first in the walk and then in trot. The renvers makes exactly the same demands from the horse as the travers which he has already mastered apart from the fact that the renvers is executed without the assistance of the wall to control the alignment of the forehand.

In a renvers the quarters remain on the track while the forehand is brought in or held in so that the forelegs move along an inner and parallel track, the horse remaining bent towards the direction of the movement. An interesting movement for both rider and horse is to alternate the renvers with the shoulder-in. This is an exercise that demands considerable finesse in the adjustment of all the aids by the rider and is a very demanding test of attention and obedience by the horse. It should not, of course, be attempted until the simple renvers on its own account has been satisfactorily learned, and it should then be practised for quite a long time in the walk before it is attempted in the trot, as the slower gait provides more time for the two partners in the operation to accomplish the change in the bend, in the leg aids, in the rein aids, and in the seat aids. It cannot fail to improve the understanding and co-ordination of the aids for the horse and the rider.

Laterals on circles

As a means of further developing the suppleness and controllability of our young horse, a start should now be made on practising lateral movements on a circle. A circle of about twelve metres is suitable for this purpose, and we can start with the shoulder-in and the travers or quarters-in, both for only a few steps at a time to begin with, then reverting to one-track work on the same circle. It will be as well to defer trying the renvers on the circle till some later stage as in that movement the joints of the hind legs, moving around the outer or larger circle, are put under considerable strain. The shoulder-in and the travers will present no great problems, though care must be taken to keep the quarters in the former and the forehand in the latter on their proper alignment in relation to the circular track. In particular, the rider must resist the temptation to push the quarters too far in in the travers as this would interfere with the ability of the forelegs to move freely round the track. And in both movements the forehand must be mainly positioned and controlled by the outside rein.

Simple changes

We have already been practising changes of leg in the canter through the trot and the walk, and it is now time to work on the perfection of the true simple change of leg, that is to say a change of leg that is achieved with at the most only three steps of walk and with the transitions into and out of the walk being achieved without any suggestion of trot. This is not at all easy and indeed is virtually impossible unless the canter is well balanced and well controlled. The rider must work at the canter with the aim of slowing down the tempo a little so that he can feel each stride, or three-time beat, as a separate entity at his disposal. He must sit up with his head well poised on his shoulders and thrust his stomach forward with each stride so that his seat will create the impulsion into his hand that alone will give him the control that he requires. As this control improves, so he will be able to slip more and more smoothly into the walk, will feel each and every step of the walk, and, mainly by a slight adjustment of his seat, strike off smoothly but energetically and clearly into the first stride of the new canter.

The reins need to be held fairly short for this or indeed for any other difficult exercise, as otherwise it will be difficult to prevent the horse from falling into the walk. The effectiveness of the balance into and out of the walk, and the degree of responsiveness of the horse to the new canter aid will both be of very great importance when we come, in perhaps six months' time, to teach the flying change of leg. The fewer the number of walk strides needed for a simple change, the easier will come the flying changes.

It is always important to maintain and develop freedom in all the gaits, and so we should balance the more collected canter that is required for simple changes with plenty of medium canter which we should demand from the horse without loss of horizontality. This is best achieved by not letting the reins become long and by the rider not allowing his body to fall in front of the vertical. He must strive to lengthen the stride by the forward urges of his seat and the small of his back.

Counter canter

Canter work at this stage should also include the counter canter on wide bends or large circles which should only be reduced as the collected canter improves. No useful purpose is served by working in counter canter in a sloppy or unbalanced manner. The need to practise the counter canter as a test of discipline to ensure that the horse will not try to change his leading leg unless specifically requested to do so should not be overplayed. Few horses will give much trouble in that respect so long as their balance is sufficiently well established, and it is possible that too much disciplined counter canter at this stage may inhibit the horse's ability to learn the flying change when its turn comes.

In trot we should by now have achieved a suppleness that will permit an eight-metre circle in collection. That, at any rate, should be our aim.

Asking the young horse for extension. Miss Farlow on Snap Happy.

CHAPTER TWELVE

Introducing Extensions
Phase 7 (Months 19–21)

Extended trot. Inside leg response. Canter half pass.
10 m canter circles. Half-halts.

As we enter the penultimate phase of our two-year programme we shall have a fairly clear idea of the general ability and special talents of our horse, and perhaps the main worry at the back of our mind will be the question of whether we have made a good job of the task of training him as a riding horse. In the six preceding phases we will have covered most of the really important lessons with the exception of the flying changes, though there will no doubt be plenty of room for further improvement in much of the work. The outline syllabus for this phase contains only two new items of major importance and, in fact, both of them, the extended trot and the canter half pass, are in effect only developments of lessons already learned. The extended trot develops naturally from the extensions already practised in medium trot, and the canter half pass follows exactly the same rules as the trot half pass.

We are thus free to expend most of our time and energies in this seventh phase in an even more comprehensive recapitulation of all the past work, with special attention and emphasis on the basic matters of suppleness, freedom and impulsion. We should carefully and rigorously test all these matters afresh with a firm determination to root out and overcome any weaknesses by fundamentally correct methods. We must not grudge a moment of the time spent on this work which we should have been doing all along but never more importantly than now.

We may increase the frequency of work on the lunge for a week or two in order to check on the freedom of the paces and to get a clear mental picture of the horse in action. At the same time we shall be confirming the horse's attention and obedience, and his willingness to give himself proudly to his work. If we find that he lunges less well than he used to and is more awkward to handle, we can be sure that we have been wrong about the soundness of the progress we had made.

We should confirm to our satisfaction that we can make the horse stretch himself to the fullest extent in all three paces whenever we want him to. We should be able to change from a collected posture to one that is long and low though still lightly on the bit. We should also be able to maintain that posture for quite a long time as a means of ensuring that the horse's back is not set but supple, submissive and able to transmit the impulsion from the quarters through to the neck and shoulders. This is an exercise that we must employ quite frequently.

We may thoroughly overhaul the half-halt system to confirm once more that each one goes right through the horse, without resistance, to link the aids of the reins, the seat and the legs. In doing this we inevitably re-establish the horse's responsiveness to the aids and in particular to the demands of the rider's inside leg applied on the girth.

Of course, we keep working away to maintain and improve on our ability to perform all the other lessons and exercises that we have been studying. The horse should by now be able to perform them all with a considerable degree of ease and fluency. Riding him should be a real pleasure, though we must not expect to get that pleasure without paying for it in terms of fairly continuous activity on our part. And we are still a very long way from the stage when we can seriously hope that the horse will do all that is asked of him to perfection. Indeed that happy dream may never materialize with any horse no matter how prolonged his education. Occasionally it may appear to a spectator to be happening like that, but the rider will almost always know better.

Extended trot

Of the two new lessons for this phase we will consider the extended trot first. This is a movement that looks as if it ought to be easy to achieve but is very often decidedly the reverse. To make it even more tantalizing, some horses will show a quite precocious ability to extend in the very early stages of their ridden education, when they still move with all the suppleness of youth and untouched nature, but then seem quite suddenly to lose that ability and to be unable to regain it for many months. But patient, correct training and a refusal to lose hope will produce at least a reasonably satisfactory result in the end.

The true essence of an extended trot is that the length of the stride should increase significantly beyond that of the working or even of the medium trot without any speeding up of the tempo. In fact, the tempo, due to the extra time spent in suspension as a result of the longer stride, may even give the impression of being a little slower. Such a slowing down of the tempo would not qualify for perfection, but it would be the lesser of the evils and would not be seriously detrimental, provided only that the horse was honestly working forward and covering ground, the leading foot following the line of its toe to the ground. It must never hesitate or appear to be drawn back from its point of maximum extension towards its point of impact with the ground.

Invariably a good extended trot is the direct outcome of the degree of perfection of the trot that preceded it. It will never be produced by itself out of a bad previous pace. In particular the previous trot must be well balanced, light and keen (the latter word being used in the sense that the horse should convey to the rider the clear impression that he has plenty of spare energy and is waiting to be shown how and where to use it). In short, he must be working with impulsion to the bit. Provided the preparatory trot contains those three qualities, the rider can expect only to have to lengthen his legs, increase the pressure of the leg aids well forward on the girth, brace his back by pressing the pelvis forward with a slightly arched but still flexible spine, and very slightly ease the restraining tension on the reins in order to get at least a few extended paces. If he gets them he should be satisfied and revert immediately to collection. He should avoid pressing on until, as will almost invariably happen, the horse begins to lose his balance, fall on to his forehand and, consequently, shorten the pace and hurry the tempo. Little and often is far, far the best motto and should be practised until the horse virtually tells the rider that he is ready and willing to continue the extension for a longer distance.

With most horses the rider will find it much more difficult to sit smoothly in the saddle in extension than in the shorter forms of trot. The greater thrust of the horse's quarters makes greater demands on the suppleness and control of the rider's back and loins. Nevertheless, the rider must strive to ride the movement and should not evade it by tilting his body either in front of or behind the vertical. The former evasion results in the seat bones ceasing to have any influence on the horse as well as causing the forehand to be loaded. The latter results in at least some extra weight being placed on the horse's loins at the very time when a free swing of the whole back is most urgently needed.

The problem of sitting comfortably through an extended trot can only be solved by the combined suppleness and strength of the backs of the two parties concerned. If the horse's back becomes so stiff and hard that it cannot be sat on, then the horse has not been adequately prepared for this movement, and it should not be attempted until the necessary corrections have been made. If the rider cannot sit quietly in extension on a supple horse, then he himself should look elsewhere for means of improving his own bodily functions to the necessary extent.

It is usually helpful if a few paces of extension are asked for several times in succession from the same marker in an arena or point in a field. This makes use of the horse's well-developed powers of anticipation so that he will prepare himself for the extra surge of impulsion required as the point is approached. Then it will be necessary to keep the anticipation under control by every now and again riding the same track without the extension. It is also psychologically helpful to both horse and rider to set a clearly visible limit to the distance to be covered in extension by having another visible marker as the point at which the trot is once more reduced to a working or collected pace. The knowledge that the tremendous effort required will not be of indefinite duration, that the end is in sight, is encouraging to both parties.

Canter half pass

The canter half pass does not require much explanation. In essence it follows all the same rules as the half pass in trot: some collection, correct positioning at the start, a lead from the inside hand, obedience from the quarters, and control by the outside rein and inside leg. The rider sits central in the saddle with a long outside leg, leaning very slightly in the direction of the movement.

The canter half pass should be practised only with some discretion to the side on which the horse tends to be crooked in canter, as it does in itself have a tendency to increase the suppleness and lateral bend on the side to which it is moving. A horse that tends to be crooked in the right canter usually has a tendency to drift to the right when he ought to be going straight, and obviously the half pass will give him an excuse to accentuate the drift. It can only be overcome by riding the right canter with an element of right shoulder-in to keep the quarters correctly on the appropriate track, and by doing many exercises to stretch and supple the opposite or left side so that, with two hopefully equal sides, the horse will have less inclination to evade straightness.

Because of the mechanics of the horse's locomotion, the canter half pass is in some ways easier for him than the trot half pass. This is because the whole thrust to the side for a complete three-beat stride is provided by the initiating or outside hind leg. One sideways thrust, and the job is done, and done by the only leg that can effectively propel the whole body sideways. The forelegs have only very limited powers of propulsion in any direction, and the inside hind leg almost none to its own side. In the trot, the outside hind leg can only act for its own diagonal, leaving the inside hind leg and outside foreleg to do their limited best for the other diagonal. The fact that it works pretty well in practice is an indication of what a clever animal the horse is and an argument in favour of those who think that it is unnecessary to worry one's head about mechanical theory.

One of the best exercises for improving the suppleness on the stiff side of the horse is the counter canter on that leg. The smaller the circle or curve on which it is carried out, the more powerful the remedial effect. This effect can be even further increased by practising the canter renvers on a circle, the bend of the renvers itself accentuating the effect of the counter canter on the quarters but helping to prevent the forehand from falling out.

Quarter pirouettes

Throughout this phase, normal work on the canter should continue with a view to improving the horse's control and co-ordination of this always difficult foot sequence and to increase his powers of collection without loss of fluency. Very short but very frequent spells of intermittent collection and lengthening are the best means of doing this, and a tentative beginning can be made in asking for quarter pirouettes from the collected periods when the latter can be carried out with really shortened steps. If these quarter pirouettes are attempted the rider must never, never try to pull the horse round with the inside rein. He must himself continue to sit very upright with a full share of weight on his outside seat bone, both hands taken a little to the inside but controlling the movement almost entirely between the outside rein and the inside leg. Any effort to use too much inside rein will be disastrous and end in the horse losing confidence and beginning to rush round with uncontrolled quarters.

Ten-metre canter circles

Ten-metre circles should be aimed at in canter, taking special care that the quarters do not fall in as they may do if the horse is finding that degree of bend too difficult for him in this gait.

The moment of request for a flying change of leg from left to right.
The author on Peter Jones.

CHAPTER THIRTEEN

Final Stages
Phase 8 (Months 22–24)

Extended canter. Double bridle. Flying changes.

We now enter the final three months of our allotted schedule, and the job we set ourselves nearly two years ago is nearly done. For the last time we remind ourselves of the vital and perpetual need to run through and check the simple, basic work which, in effect, means suppling the horse and putting him to the aids. This preliminary work must always be done thoroughly and wholeheartedly, with as much interest and attention as if the lesson was being taught for the very first time, or else it will be of no effect. It may take four or five minutes, or it may need fifteen or even twenty minutes before we are satisfied. The time will depend on the changing moods and physical condition of the horse and of the rider, both living beings subject to change.

We shall have the feeling that we are running up to an examination to be held at the end of this phase. There may be no examiners other than ourselves, but the final result of our labours will be no less acutely scrutinized for that, and careful revision is the best note to end on. But the coming examination will not be final because, as interested and relatively educated horsemen, we shall continue improving our horse, if only in little ways, for most of his working life, depending on what form that is likely to take.

If he is destined by now to move into the sphere of advanced dressage, he has a long way to go and many things to learn. If he is going to take part in eventing or high-level show jumping he will benefit by all the training he has so far absorbed and some more besides, including the two items which we shall be introducing in this eighth and last phase of the programme. So, whichever way things go, we continue to work with an open-ended and unflagging enthusiasm.

Extended canter

The simpler of the last two additions to our vocabulary will be the extended canter, and we can deal with it quite shortly in much the same way as we dealt with the canter half pass in the previous phase. That is to say, we work on exactly the same basis as we used for the similar lesson in trot. We first strive to improve the balance, rhythm and impulsion of the preliminary canter, be it collected, working or medium; we check the rider's position, balance, depth of seat and suppleness; and we ask by a clasping leg aid and a bracing of the back for the maximum extension that we can obtain without increasing the tempo or falling below the horizontal line of balance. We do this for comparatively short spells and for short distances so that the horse will not lose his concentration. It will nevertheless be beneficial now and again to give him a quite long stint of extended canter, or even a steady gallop, to stretch the appropriate muscles and to remind him of his tremendous potential in this direction. Really powerful, free movement of this kind will do much to release any underlying tensions and frustrations and will help to keep him fresh, alert, and willing to go forward from the leg or, preferably, from the seat influence alone.

Flying changes

The final and the most fascinating item on our curriculum is the lesson of the flying change of leg in canter. Probably no other accomplishment adds more to the pleasure of riding than the ability to perform a quiet, discreet, smooth and effortless flying change whenever the occasion or the whim of the moment demands it. It is so neat, so extraordinarily efficient and so wonderfully clever on the part of the horse.

Every horse in a state of unencumbered freedom can and will perform flying changes without the slightest difficulty as and when it pleases him when in the field. And virtually every horse, except possibly those with the dullest of minds, can be taught to perform them when carrying a rider and at the precise request of the rider. Nevertheless, and with very few exceptions on both sides of the partnership, the business of actually teaching the first lessons in flying changes is seldom easy and is often fraught with difficulty and anxiety. It can never be treated lightly and expected to happen in the same way as that in which a horse which has mastered leg-yielding and shoulder-in can be expected to respond almost automatically to the aids for half pass, even if the rider has had considerable previous experience. The rider who has never ridden flying changes before would be well advised to make some arrangement whereby he can become thoroughly acquainted with them on a trained horse before trying to teach them to a young one. In short, the rider must have confidence in his own ability if he is to avoid the risk of serious misunderstandings with his horse.

There are two underlying reasons for the potential complications. First is the fact, often forgotten, that the loose horse in the field does his changes without any conscious thought. He is totally unconscious of what he is doing or of what locomotory adjustments he has to make in order to perform the act. The change is a natural reflex, an action conditioned by the circumstances of the moment, in the same way as a swallow will make a miraculous turn in the air to catch an insect. The free horse will change to relieve the strain on certain muscles or to get round a corner more easily. In neither case will he be conscious of what he has done nor how he did it. Now, however, he has to learn to change in a fully controlled, deliberate and thoughtful manner in co-operation with the whim of his rider only.

The second underlying reason, not unconnected with the first, is concerned with the extremely accurate timing that has to be mastered by the rider and synchronized with the mechanical reflexes of the horse. The change, say from canter-left to canter-right, involves a complete reversal of the four-leg sequence, and this reorganization can only take place during the exceedingly brief period of time when all four legs are off the ground and therefore free and able to be reorganized. This free period is, of course, the period immediately after the third beat of the canter, the period of total suspension. But in order to make it possible for this marvellous thing to take place in this brief moment that is almost too brief to be seen by the untrained eye, the instruction has to be sent well in advance to allow for the nervous, mental and physical reactions that must occur, though not so early as to risk interfering with the previous stride. Clearly all this allows no room for any clumsy fumbling on the part of the rider who must, on the contrary, be able to act with knowledge, confidence and precision.

Having outlined the problems, we can reassure ourselves that they involve nothing that cannot be mastered by any reasonably competent horseman and that our horse, having got this far, will certainly not be that half-witted nag that will never make a decent flying change. So let us proceed with this most interesting of all the lessons.

Defining the flying change

The key to the flying change lies, as with virtually everything else in equitation, in the hind quarters. It is the quarters that must initiate the change, and if they do so correctly the rest will follow. To be more precise the change is initiated by one hind leg which has a very special job to do and which is worth a moment's special study so that we know exactly what we have to bring about.

We will imagine we want to change from canter-right to canter-left. The canter-right is initiated at each stride by the left hind leg with the right hind leg coming forward as part of the second or diagonal beat. If we think only of the hind legs, the sequence of each successive stride will be left–right, left–right, left–right. But now, during the moment of suspension that follows one chosen stride, the right hind leg has to accelerate its motion in the air so that it will pass the also suspended left hind leg and come forward to the ground first instead of second. The left hind leg then follows through with a prolonged and lengthened swing in the air to become the second beat, with its corresponding diagonal foreleg, of the new canter-left. The landing of the remaining left foreleg completes the change. The hind leg sequence will now be right–left, right–left, right–left.

There is seldom any real difficulty about the change to be carried out by the forelegs. If we concentrate on the hind legs, the forelegs will to all intents look after themselves, though naturally we must be aware of what they are doing so that we can be ready to help if some temporary relatively minor problem does occur. Should we be so ill-advised as to concentrate on the forelegs, we shall risk starting the very bad habit of changing his forelegs before the hind legs, a habit which is exceedingly difficult to eradicate.

Having got quite clear in our minds just what has to be done, or rather just what the horse has to do to make a flying change, we have then to devise some way of getting him to do it. By no stretch of the imagination can we actually make him do it, short of using some sort of quite unacceptable brute force that would defeat our object by frightening him. Rather, we have to devise and use one or more simple aids or signals that are most likely to induce the required result in the locomotory adjustment. In the simplest terms, that means causing the old number two hind leg to become the new number one, thereby taking on the job of initiating the new canter.

Execution of the flying change

There are many theories on the best method of approach to the point where the rider first asks for a flying change from his young horse. It will depend in each case to some extent on the temperament and talent of the horse but also on the whims and previous experience of the rider. There is no one foolproof approach, but all will share the vital necessity of not being put to the test until or unless the canter–walk and the walk–canter transitions are as refined and as near perfect as possible. That will ensure that the canter is well balanced, well co-ordinated and responsive. If we endeavour to get flying changes without those qualifications we shall be asking for trouble and disappointment.

Of all the many methods advocated in the books and the teaching of experts, we will choose for our young horse the simplest of all, and the one that follows most closely to the preparation work that we have just been discussing. There will come a day when we decide that it is time to attempt it and, if it turns out to be a day on which things seem to be going right, we shall take courage and put our skills to this great and exciting test. Having suppled the horse in the usual manner and put him to the aids we shall, while he is still fresh and keen, go on to a large circle and practise a series of strike-offs from the walk, varying the leading leg in an irregular sequence so that the horse has to pay attention and cannot anticipate. We continue with this work for five or ten minutes with only sufficient breaks to ensure that the horse does not tire, or until he is giving good, bold strike-offs in immediate response to clear, firm but strictly correct aids. Spurs should not be worn, for reasons that will become clear later. We want the canter to be bold, active, just a little more collected than the working gait, and full of impulsion. We should use our seat strongly so as to discourage any shortening of the stride.

When we are satisfied with the canter and the strike-offs, we place ourselves on whichever rein is consistent with the most supple side of the horse. If the horse is softer on the right side than the left, we go to the right circle, and move in counter canter with the left lead. We are going to ask the horse to give us a flying change from the difficult or outside lead to the easy and more comfortable inside lead. That way he will perhaps try a little harder to accommodate us. We have chosen the right rein on the circle because it will be a little easier for the horse to swing the right hind leg, the leg on his soft side, through to the front to become the second instead of the first beat in the new canter.

We will also explain at this point why we have decided to use the circle to teach the first lesson in flying changes, instead of one of the other systems that advocate asking for the change from a figure of eight, or from a counter canter just before the corner after the long side of an arena, or on re-joining the track after a half circle – or indeed any method which involves a distinct change of direction closely connected to the actual change. We have chosen the circle method because it is just that change of direction that we want to avoid. In one sense the change of direction should make it easier for the horse to understand the logic of the change and perhaps even to make the mechanical adjustment necessary to perform it. But it can also unquestionably lead to trouble in that it introduces the element of anticipation and may result in the horse throwing himself into the new direction and on to his shoulder. The former is always highly undesirable, and the latter puts the horse off balance and may end in his changing in front but not behind which is the greatest of all the bugbears of flying changes. The undesirability of anticipation by a horse lies mainly in the fact that it is a form of dis-obedience that is annoying and disturbing to the rider's own plans, but it also usually ends in the horse becoming nervous and unsteady in his rhythm.

By working on the circle we avoid both these major risks. We have the added advantage of being able to work in a continuous manner without the interruptions inevitably caused by the negotiation of sharp corners or of having to wait for our next try for a change until we reach some predetermined point in the school or arena. We can ask for a change whenever we feel that the omens are auspicious with the horse attentive and balanced. There are no markers to tell him when to expect or anticipate this strange new request. There are no sharp corners that he has to negotiate at the same time or immediately after he has done his best to respond to what must seem to him to be an incomprehensible and difficult question. In short, it is the author's opinion that the circular method provides by far the best chance of tackling successfully and calmly a problem that usually requires a great deal of tact and skill if a build-up of tensions of one sort or another is to be avoided.

Getting back to the job at hand, we must concentrate on feeling the three clear beats of the canter as we proceed in counter canter on the right rein. What we then propose to do is, at the appropriate moment, to change our position in the saddle and our canter aids from those appropriate for canter-left to those required for canter-right. We have to make that adjustment just before the very brief moment of suspension between the last beat of one canter stride and the first beat of the next.

We should try to be very precise in our movement and timing rather than abrupt or sudden, but to begin with it will be advisable to make the outer leg aid a good deal more forceful than we normally do for a strike-off. In all other respects it will be the same. We must take care not to frighten or upset the horse, but we can afford to surprise him a little bit so that he jumps to the command a little more briskly and determinedly than usual. With that mental jump may come the jump through with the hind legs that we need, but we must at all costs avoid giving the aid so forcefully that he jumps sideways away from it instead of forwards.

It is not possible to predict exactly how each or any horse will react to the early requests for a change of leg, or what each rider will have to do to overcome the many subtle problems that will inevitably arise from these reactions. With luck and good preparatory training those problems will be small and can be ironed out with common sense, sympathy and tact. A little stronger or clearer aid with the leg, a little more give with the new inside hand, or perhaps a little more or a little less weight on the seat bones may be necessary. So much must depend on the rider's skill, knowledge, sympathy and sense of feel. For the moment we can only try to ensure that the dice are at least loaded in our favour by giving ourselves a mental refresher about the fundamental aspects of riding that are involved in the actual execution of this exercise and which will, other things being equal, be most likely to bring success to our efforts to teach the flying changes.

The rider, in the approach to the change, should sit high and light so as to avoid interfering with the free working of the horse's back. The contact with the seat bones must be smooth and unbroken.

The rider should take special pains to clasp the body of the horse with his legs as far round the barrel as possible, with the toes kept well to the front, so that he can maintain the most sensitive feel of the movements of the horse. It will also allow the horse to maintain the most sensitive feel of the movements of the rider's seat and legs and so be the quicker to understand and respond to them. Keeping the toes to the front will help to ensure that the legs are relaxed and that the horse does not become anxious about spurs.

The rider must strive to maintain a good flowing impulsion right up to and through the change so that the momentum of the horse will prevent any hesitation in the stride, reducing the period of suspension and so making it more difficult to make the change.

While restraining any tendency to rush, the rider must be very careful to ensure that the horse does not feel himself to be restricted by any action of the hands. They must not exert any backward pull and must be able to follow and encourage the impulsive thrust of the hind legs and, in particular, of the hind legs in the act of changing. The importance of this is connected with the fact already mentioned that, in the actual stride of the change, the new inside hind leg has to make a more than usually prolonged jump in terms both of time and of distance covered.

Finally, the rider should remember that, in a change from canter-left to canter-right, the most important thing is to accelerate the movement, forward and to the ground, of the left hind leg which will initiate the new canter. For that purpose the rider's best tool is his left seat bone, which should therefore on no account be allowed to lose its contact with the saddle. If the change is achieved, the predominance must immediately be transferred to the right or new inside seat bone. The actual aid for the change, initiated by the left seat bone, will include the almost simul-taneous withdrawal of the left leg to its new position behind the girth, with a strong inward pressure as if to say 'now', and the forward move-ment of the right leg to its new position on the girth, where it will immediately act to maintain straightness and impulsion in the right canter. In making these movements, both legs must slide along the horse's ribs so that he can clearly feel them moving and will not be taken unawares by the sudden final pressure that says 'now'.

If we go about things in this way we should theoretically obtain a correct flying change from our horse at the first time of asking. But to expect that degree of success may be trying our luck too far and it is more probable that most of us will achieve something more like a general fumble the first time; a change of sorts, not necessarily correct both behind and in front, at the second or third try; and then, having tested the ground and got the feel of the horse's reactions, a fairly good change with perhaps some loss of balance and a little plunge forward. We should not be anything but pleased so long as, after the first or second try, the horse does make a definite effort to change. If that happens, we can rest assured that it will only need a little perseverance and we shall be home and dry. The great thing is to have obtained a definite and co-operative, even if an erratic, response from the horse. We then know that the penny is dropping. We continue to ask only for the change from left to right.

We may or may not get the response we hope for the first time, or even the second or third time. But if we feel that the horse has under-stood and has tried to respond, even though his powers of co-ordination have failed him, that will have been a worthwhile beginning. On no account must we become irritated or unduly despondent. We have to keep trying, always asking ourselves whether we are giving the horse a fair chance by giving our aids correctly and timely, and sooner or later we shall succeed. We may not succeed the first day to the extent that we do not achieve even one true flying change, or even a recognizable effort at a change. That would not be any great surprise to any but the most talented and experienced riders. We should not then continue to demand the change more than perhaps ten or fifteen times without any result. To repeat indefinitely our obviously incomprehensible request will eventually upset both horse and rider, and to end the lesson on that note would be the greatest disaster of all. If we are clearly not achieving any result, we should stop and reassure ourselves that both parties will have learnt something as a useful basis for another try the next day. If, after two or three days, we have still got negligible results we should then face up to the regrettable fact that our preparation work has not been good enough with either the horse or the rider, and we should put flying changes out of our mind until we have remedied that situation. But sooner or later we shall assuredly achieve our object.

If we can get one, or at the most two, reasonably clear-cut changes we must be satisfied, make very much of the horse, jump off his back, give him a tit-bit, and take him back to the stable. Indeed, we must make an absolute point of giving the horse several pats immediately after his every co-operative effort to change, and then return to the walk for a short rest, with more pats. It is important that the first pats should come within a second of the change or effort to change, without waiting to slow down to the walk, as it is vital that the horse should be aware that his half-conscious effort to do this strange thing is met with strong approval. In that way he will remain calm and relaxed, which of course is essential. It is also essential that we should resist the temptation to 'do a few more' or to insist too much that at least one change must be perfect before the lesson can finish. Either of those things is far too liable to result in the lesson finishing with tempers a little bit frayed, with a mutual lack of confidence, and with the horse mentally and physically overtaxed. We would go back to his stable with an unhappy memory of the whole business that would sour all subsequent lessons for a considerable time with possibly lasting ill-effects.

We should work at the flying changes for a short, calm but energetic session each day for several days or perhaps a week. Always we generously reward every bit of success or improvement with pats and periods of walk. And we keep strictly to the left–right change. By the end of the week, or earlier if success has come smoothly, it will be wise to give it a rest for several days. If all is going well the break from the rather special strains of this lesson will pay off. On the other hand, if our achievement has been less than satisfactory, or at best erratic, the rest will be equally or even more beneficial to soothe the frayed nerves and perhaps aching muscles. But after a few days' rest we can start again in the same quiet way. If the initial sessions have produced satisfactory and reliable changes from left to right, it will now be safe to start on those from right to left. But it is not wise to do this while there still exists any uncertainty about the others, as to mix them in the early stages might cause confusion.

Perfecting flying changes

We chose to start with the changes from the stiff-side canter to the soft-side canter because it should be easier for the horse. Therefore we must not be surprised if this second stage is more difficult, just because the horse finds it more difficult. It is not uncommon to find that whereas the changes to the easier side have been achieved with pleasing speed and ease, the changes to the other side take some weeks, or even months, to achieve with anything like comparable efficiency. But we need not anticipate that trouble and must ride the lesson with all the confidence and precision that we can muster.

Once we can get the changes to either side with reasonable assurance and fluency, we should begin to concentrate on reducing any degree of fierceness or of excessive movement that may have crept into our leg aids in the effort to get the early changes. Above all else we want the changes to be straight, which means that the quarters must show no tendency to swing to the side of the new lead. For that reason we should not neglect the part played by the rider's new inside leg which will help, in a shoulder-in fashion, to keep the forehand in front of the quarters as the change is made. A good change should be as smooth as a knife going through butter and as straight as if all four legs were moving along closely parallel tramlines. To achieve such a change is never easy with a young horse, and it may become even more difficult as the horse becomes accustomed to the game and at the same time begins to learn ways of evading some of the muscular stresses involved. We should be on our guard against such evasions, which almost always involve crookedness of some kind. Our ideal should therefore be to ride our changes with the lightest possible aids and with as little visible movement of the legs as possible.

Throughout the whole of this phase, which means to the end of the period under review in this book, we should be well advised to restrict our work on flying changes to those done on the big circle or absolutely straight lines. It will be tempting to try them in connection with various figures, but all such figures introduce a certain risk of anticipation and of hesitation at the moment of the change, both of which can cause grave problems and hinder progress. A half circle with flying change on rejoining the track is also very liable, due to the element of anticipation, to tempt the horse to be crooked as he sidles a little towards the track. The maintenance of continuous impulsion is of such importance in the long-term development and perfection of the changes that it is far better to stick to the simple changes until they are thoroughly established and so fully absorbed into the vocabulary that they create no shadow of anxiety to horse or rider. If all is going well and the rider is confident of his ability, some further interest can be introduced quite safely by beginning to repeat the changes after a fixed number of strides. Six or eight would be a good number to start with, depending on the speed with which the horse becomes totally steady and balanced again after each change. These tempo changes are an excellent and telling test of that balance.

Double bridle

The last thing we should discuss in this final phase of the two-year programme is the use of the double bridle. But before we go into any detail it must be clearly understood that a double bridle should never be used in any phase of training or for any specific exercise until and unless that work has been well covered and can be well performed in a snaffle. The snaffle is the bit in which every aspect of the horse's education, without exception, should be taught in the first instance. That refers particularly to the ability of the horse to maintain a correct balance at all times. The double bridle is the bit which can then be used, like the final coat of paint, to put the gloss on the well-prepared foundation. Everything that really matters can be achieved in the snaffle, and any weak spots in that achievement will – to use the paint analogy again – show through the final gloss and will by then be very difficult to correct. In general terms, therefore, the introduction of the double bridle should always be deferred rather than expedited. The double bridle will cure no ills, it will make worse what is bad and it will add flavour to what is already good.

All the arguments against using a double bridle in the early stages of training originate from the inherent mechanical strength of the curb bit and from the unavoidable difficulty in using that strength with sufficient tact and gentleness in the many unpredictable circumstances that will inevitably arise. Resulting from those two factors, there is a grave risk of hurting or frightening the young horse or, perhaps a little short of either, of inhibiting the freedom of action of his paces and general muscular activity. It has to be faced that riders do not always have total control of their every action and reaction. It also has to be faced that young horses are quite liable to fall off balance suddenly in the middle of some exercise, thus placing a sudden increase of tension on the bit and their mouth. It would obviously be fatal if the horse were to find that some quite innocent mistake on his part, and probably one that he did not even know he had made, resulted in a sharp pain or discomfort in his mouth. Another point is that, with the best will in the world, and notwithstanding all the basic principles about never pulling on a horse's mouth, young horses are often somewhat tough and wilful and, if only in the interests of safety, are occasionally going to receive some fairly strong action from the reins. A direct pull through a thick-mouthed snaffle can be administered if need be with little fear of long-term damage, but it is impossible to calculate what may result if the same sort of pull is made through the curb bit.

Despite these cautionary words, we should be able to do some work in a double bridle before the end of our two-year programme, though it should never be thought of as having superseded the snaffle which remains the basic schooling bit. At this stage it might be wise to restrict the use of the double bridle to one or two days a week at first, and never more than three or four. But first we should give some thought about how best to introduce this comparatively complicated piece of equipment so that it will not be feared, ignored or fought against by the horse. It would be a grave mistake to substitute the double for the snaffle suddenly one morning and to expect the horse to discover for himself how it is meant to work and what part he is expected to play in its workings. We have, in short, to explain it to him.

The bridoon

The bridoon, or snaffle portion, of a double bridle works exactly like the ordinary snaffle except that it may be fitted a little higher in the mouth to make room between the teeth for the curb bit. When put to maximum use it will always tend to slide upwards in the mouth and therefore have a slight raising effect on the horse's head. The curb bit has an opposite, more complicated and much more powerful effect. These important differences should never be forgotten by the rider if the horse is not to be confused. Theoretically, the two reins should be used quite separately, and indeed this is perfectly possible if the two bridoon reins are held in one hand and the two curb reins in the other. That is a useful way to hold them for certain specific exercises and in particular for making the very early introduction of the double bridle to the horse. But it is not a satisfactory method for ordinary purposes, as it is too clumsy and almost impossible to apply an opening rein. Therefore, we have to settle for a compromise, each hand holding the two reins on its own side with priority given to the contact of the bridoon.

Many horses will display noticeable signs of uncertainty or nervousness when first asked to accept the two bits into their mouth. There is more steel, it is noisy, they overlap, and there is more movement than from the simple and well-known snaffle. To overcome these anxieties we will take the trouble for three or four days, just before the normal work, to put the double bridle on in the stable for about fifteen minutes, replacing it with the snaffle before we go outside to work.

Trial fittings

In the first trial fitting, the first five minutes should be spent carefully fitting the bridle. First fit the bridoon so that it creates a fairly definite wrinkle in the corners of the lips and does not sag unduly over the tongue. It must still, nevertheless, be well clear of the upper teeth. Then fit the curb bit, so that initially it lies on the bars of the mouth with about $2\frac{1}{2}$ centimetres of clearance above the tushes of a gelding, and not less than $2\frac{1}{2}$ centimetres below the point of contact of the bridoon on the bars. There will probably be quite a big margin for further adjustment within those limits, the final position then being decided by the position of the curb chain: it should lie smoothly and flat in the chin groove when hooked on so that the cheeks of the bit cannot be pulled back to an angle of more than about 35 degrees with the lips. To achieve this fitting, the curb bit may have to be raised or lowered a little by adjusting the leather headpiece until, when the curb rein is pulled tight, the curb chain falls easily into its correct place.

After giving the horse a few minutes to come to terms with his new bridle, of which the lower cheeks should not be longer than 6 to $7\frac{1}{2}$

centimetres, we set about the first lesson in its use. We do this dismounted and in the stable. It is a lesson that is far too often overlooked, with more or less evil results on the young horse's eventual acceptance and understanding of the double bridle.

Standing beside the horse's shoulder, facing forward, we take both the bridoon reins in our right hand at a point about six inches behind and under the jaw. With the left hand we take both the curb reins at a point about nine inches behind the bit. We take a firm but light contact with the bridoon reins and try to get the horse to carry his head within about five or, at most, ten degrees from the vertical. When we are satisfied and the horse is quietly paying attention, we gently take a light but steady contact with the curb rein, watching very carefully for any reaction from the horse. The reaction we don't want is that he should show any sign of moving backwards. This is not a common reaction, but if he does so we must immediately release the curb rein.

The reaction that we hope for is a relaxation or giving of the lower jaw, preferably without any parting of the lips. On the instant that we see or feel that relaxation, we release the curb pressure entirely and caress the horse. But in all probability there will be a period of mystified immobility of the jaw to begin with, in which case we may increase the curb pressure a little, though never to the point of brute force. A little patience, and perhaps a little give and take if there is prolonged resistance, will almost invariably produce the result we want within half a minute or so at the most, and the battle will have been won. We repeat the lesson three or four times, always rewarding the correct response with a caress and perhaps some sugar or a nut, before removing the bridle and proceeding with the day's work in a snaffle.

The double bridle in mounted work

After two or three days of this exercise in the stable, the lesson will have been well enough established to be repeated mounted. But before we take that step we must be certain that the relaxation of the jaw has become an immediate and almost unconscious reaction by the horse to the lever pressure of the curb bit. To ride a horse in a double bridle without any introduction is to court trouble and damage to the mouth, and even a permanent resistance to the bit. Out of doors the horse will have many other things to distract his attention, and it is all too likely that he will ignore the lever action of the bit, regarding it as an unpleasant nuisance caused by the heavy hands of the rider. If that happens he will very, very soon get the habit of stiffening his jaw against any pressure that we like to apply, either light or strong, and we shall have a ruined horse on our hands. It is, of course, perfectly possible to carry through the introductory lessons from the saddle in a satisfactory manner, but it is easier and safer to do them first in the stable, if only because there will be nothing to distract the horse's attention and because we shall have the advantage of being able to see as well as to feel. We shall, in the latter context, be able to react all the quicker to the horse's response.

The early mounted lessons are best done in the vicinity of the stable when the bridle can be removed after ten or fifteen minutes and normal work continued in a snaffle. Alternatively, we can take the horse for a really quiet hack during which we can repeat the lesson several times at a slow walk, so that there is no likelihood of the horse losing his balance, riding him in between on the bridoon rein alone and virtually dropping the curb rein. There should certainly be no cantering and preferably no trotting, either of which might excite the horse and result in an undesirable use of the bridle on an already rather anxious mouth.

After perhaps a week of this work we shall have established sufficient confidence to be able to leave the double bridle in position for all normal work for perhaps one or two days a week to begin with. It will be as well to restrict its use to the collected walk only, and to the beginning of the day's work when the horse is not tired and will have the least tendency to lean on the hand. But in any work in which the horse is likely to become excited, we must be very careful to use the bridoon alone. In any case, the curb rein must be used with extreme discretion for many weeks and should be positively used only on rare occasions. The horse will then come to respect it without fear or anxiety.

If we proceed in this careful and methodical way we shall have no problems, provided we always take special pains to ensure that the curb bit and chain are never tightened except when we deliberately cause it to happen. The tightening of the fingers must always be the minimum necessary, and it must be released immediately it is acknowledged by the relaxation of the jaw. To achieve that relaxation is the sole purpose of the curb bit. It is not there to stop or even to check the horse for which, at the stage of equitation under discussion, we should rely on the snaffle as before. But the lever action of the curb is much more powerful than is sometimes realized, and unless it is used with discretion and some expertise it is bound to have at least a checking effect, and at worst it will alarm and therefore cause resistance in the horse. Once the horse acquires the habit of resisting, the result can only be a perpetual tug-of-war, with ever-increasing strength being used on both sides, and that is obviously not the purpose of using a double bridle.

For all normal work, and provided the bit is fitted correctly, it will virtually operate itself by the mere weight of the rein. Unless we wish to send a special message through the curb bit, we can to all intents and purposes use our hands as if they only held the bridoon.

The most commonly practised method of holding the reins of a double bridle is with the bridoon rein outside the little finger of each hand and with the curb rein between the little and the third finger. That method ensures that the bridoon receives the strongest contact and is most affected by any turning or bending of the wrist. There are other methods that can be used for special purposes, and more especially for the early introductory lessons already described when it is desirable to separate as much as possible the actions of the two bits, but most of them need not be considered within the scope of this book.

As we go through all the old exercises and figures with the double bridle, we have to pay special attention to ensure that the horse always works up to the bit and does not hold back in fear of it. The slightest tendency to drop behind it must immediately be discouraged by more active driving aids and, if necessary, by allowing greater freedom of the stride. It is worth checking every now and again that the reins are still being held correctly and that the main contact is still on the bridoon. Most importantly, the horse should be ridden frequently and actively in a plain snaffle, however advanced his training, to maintain full, free, forward movement.

We can end this discussion of the double bridle by suggesting that it must never be regarded or used as a way out of a difficulty or as a panacea to cure ills. Rather it is used somewhat like a Sunday suit on a well-washed body to give a touch of elegance to a special occasion or performance. All the foundation work of all lessons should invariably be done on the snaffle because that excellent bit is the least likely to distract or disturb a horse that may be having difficulty in learning some lesson and in maintaining his balance the while.

If, by the end of this eighth phase and twenty-fourth month we can ride our horse happily and quietly in a double bridle through all the paces and movements that have been discussed, we can be satisfied that we have made a good riding horse and one that will be able to make the best of his natural abilities whatever the activity he is asked to take part in.

Afterword

The study of equitation is a matter of infinite variety and detail. It follows that the great books on the subject, intended for frequent reference over the whole spectrum of at least one of the main disciplines, are inevitably quite long and are so full of detail that they often suffer a certain amount of neglect after the first reading by those who take a somewhat light-hearted view of their equitational studies.

The present volume has strictly limited horizons and is intended for use as a handy guide book along one clearly defined path for readers who want to avoid getting held up by overlong theoretical discussions or by the sheer quantity of reading matter. The author has therefore attempted to restrict the subject matter of the book to the absolute essentials necessary for the achievement of the target: the production of a well-trained riding horse. For this reason quite a number of aspects of horse training that might be expected to be included have been discussed lightly or not at all.

Jumping has not been mentioned although it is good gymnastic training, as well as being an enjoyable activity, for any young horse. It can certainly be introduced with advantage into the sort of training programme that we have in mind, at first over cavaletti on the lunge, and then free over rather larger fences if a school or jumping lane is available. Mounted jumping over cavaletti and small jumps can become part of the curriculum towards the end of the first year once the horse has established his ability to carry himself and his rider with ease and in balance and is fully obedient to the rein and leg aids. Great care must always be taken to organize and practise all jumping in such a way that the horse remains absolutely calm and attentive with no inclination to rush on or to go above the bit. Provided these elementary precautions are taken, jumping can do nothing but good to stretch and elasticate the muscles and to improve the balance in the most natural manner. Virtually all horses enjoy jumping, and so it also acts as a form of mental relaxation from the more concentrated daily schooling.

Hacking. Relaxation from routine schooling immediately raises the question of the value of hacking in the fields and lanes, if such facilities are available which cannot nowadays be taken for granted. There seems in general, among many British riders, to be a widespread and sentimentally based idea that young horses require to be taken out for hacks several days a week if they are not to be ruined by overschooling. And yet those same people will happily send their children to school five days a week. Certainly every horse should have one day off per week, though there are many experienced horsemen who believe that even that day should not be spent entirely in the stable. So, according to personal taste and the temperament of the individual horse, the day of rest can include a quiet hack, or an hour or two loose in the paddock, or a romp in an enclosed school or manège. In considering this question, it should not be forgotten that it is an excellent thing, if possible, for the horse to stretch, relax, roll and graze in the paddock for an hour or so each and every day after his work is finished.

If, in addition to that day of complete or relative rest, the young horse is allotted one day devoted mainly to cavaletti, lungeing or hacking, he will be left with only five days of straightforward schooling per week, and that is by no means too much for any healthy young horse. Indeed, he will need it if he is to make reasonably good progress in the development of his muscle and his intelligence. We should proceed on the basis that the work of today forms the foundation of the work of tomorrow. There is no reason why the routine should be boring or lead to staleness if the trainer uses his intelligence, is aware of the possibility and adjusts the feeding to the work being done. It will be easy enough to find excuses for a few extra holidays from time to time even without the intervention of illness or other unavoidable interruptions. So work the horse, and ensure that both parties enjoy it.

Spurs. Spurs are an essential part of the tools of horsemanship but, like the carpenter's chisel, they can do a lot of harm if they are used badly, roughly or without discretion. Their purpose and use falls into three categories:

1. They can be used, on very rare occasions, as a means of punishment, in which case it should be short and sharp and quickly forgotten.
2. They are used, rather more frequently but by no means all the time, as a reminder to the horse that the quiet pressure of the booted leg is not the only sanction at the rider's disposal and should therefore not be ignored. Their very presence on the rider's heels is usually detected with uncanny speed by the horse and is usually sufficient to achieve this purpose.
3. Primarily, and most constantly, spurs are used as a refinement of the leg aids. The rider is able to be more accurate, more precise and more timely with the end of a small piece of metal than with an ill-defined expanse of leather boot.

While spurs are valuable to all horsemen, there are two powerful reservations for their use. First, spurs should never be used – at any rate by the type of rider likely to be interested in this book – during the first six months or so of a young horse's ridden education. They can all too easily be a disturbing and even frightening influence on the young animal who has many things to learn and become accustomed to, at a time when calmness is of great importance. We cannot risk making him afraid of the leg. Spurs should therefore be postponed until the horse/rider partnership and system of communication have become thoroughly established and accepted in their basic forms.

The second reservation is that spurs should not be worn by riders who are not sufficiently competent and well schooled to be certain that they never touch their horse with the spur except when they intend to do so for a specific purpose and duration of time. In the same context, the rider should be a good enough craftsman to be able to resist the temptation to use the spur on all occasions instead of the normal and more gentle aid of the booted leg. This temptation is real enough and will inevitably result in a deterioration of the rider's seat as he tends more and more to drop his toes, raise his heel and take his knee away from the saddle in his efforts to keep his spurs in constant contact with the horse. To avoid these pitfalls it is a good exercise for any rider, however experienced, to ride without spurs periodically and for a few days at a time.

However, if the rider sits correctly his spurs will not embarrass him or his horse. It can then be said that the wearing of spurs, combined with a knowledge of their dangers, can encourage the rider to maintain the essential and constant check on his seat and general techniques.

Dangers.   In looking back over the task outlined in this book, it may be helpful to highlight for a moment one or two of the dangers that are most likely to arise and have to be guarded against.

The first to be mentioned is concerned with impulsion. We know only too well that our chief aim is to achieve collection, which is the marshalling of the horse's forces: to achieve collection we have to have impulsion, brought about by the increasing engagement of the hind quarters. But it is useless and, in fact, dangerous to the success of the whole operation to go on asking for more and more activity and impulsion from the quarters, unless it can be matched by an equivalent degree of suppleness in the spine, neck and poll. Without that suppleness, the impulsion cannot be absorbed within the horse, with the result that it is either stifled at birth or, if we insist on asking for it, produces speed instead of collection. In the latter case, the stiff neck resists the restraining influence of the reins, and the stiff back does not allow the quarters to engage further forward under the mass. So we get a form of unproductive stalemate.

We are faced with the constant need to preserve a somewhat knife-edged balance between suppleness and impulsion, but with priority always going to the former. Nevertheless, this is in total conformity with the overall system of training in which, from the very beginning, we worked to loosen and supple the young horse and, only later, when we had added some muscular strength, did we begin to think about collection. Always the suppleness, throughout the length of the horse, must be first obtained and then constantly refreshed and maintained as more difficult requests are made of the horse's physique. This is best done by frequent reversion to the basic techniques of stretching the horse by working him long and low, and by the use of simple, open-ended lateral movements such as leg-yielding on straight lines and circles.

Another danger also connected with suppleness is that the rider may, in his well-intentioned efforts not to interfere directly with his horse's head carriage, let his hand become too fixed and set. If that occurs, the horse's head and mouth is also liable to become set. His jaw and poll will cease to be supple. The rider must therefore always ensure that his hands, though quiet and more or less still, remain alive and in constant communication with the horse. Then the horse will not go to sleep on them, and the rider will be able to anticipate any awkwardness or resistance to his wishes, keeping one jump ahead of his pupil.

Finally, let us remember that the training schedule recommended in this book must not be regarded as rigid or sacrosanct, nor must the rider who endeavours to follow it be unduly disappointed if he falls behind the schedule in certain respects. Rather, it should be regarded as a guide that is perfectly practical for the average rider with some ability and basic knowledge of the subject, which could certainly be improved upon in terms of timing by an experienced and accomplished rider working under ideal conditions. If the former type of rider finds that he is losing touch, he should look for the remedy within himself rather than assume that his horse is abnormally difficult. To help ensure that this situation does not arise, the less experienced rider could do worse than constantly remind himself to sit well up, to ride well forward with the stomach and the small of the back, and to keep his hands well up to the classic level. He should also remember that there is virtually no rider, however good, who will not benefit enormously by having regular visual checks on his work from a critical friend on the ground. In this way, many faults in horse or rider can be spotted in good time and appropriate steps taken to eradicate or improve them.

Note: re illustrations Recent veterinary research has shown, apparently conclusively, that the horse's spine is incapable of measurable lateral flexion between the point at which the rider sits and the tail. This factor is an important modification to all previous dressage doctrine which has taught that the spine should, when called upon, be bent uniformly from poll to tail. All relevant line-drawings in this book should be interpreted accordingly.

Glossary

BALANCE. The ability of the horse to maintain the distribution of his weight, together with that of his rider, in approximately equal proportion over all four legs.

COLLECTION. The concentration of the horse's forces, brought about by the increased engagement of the quarters with increased flexion of the joints of the hind legs.

IMPULSION. The energy from the hind quarters that passes through the horse and is controlled and directed by the rider's hands through the reins.

RHYTHM. The regularity and correctly ordered flow of the pace.

TEMPO. The rate of the stride or footfall.

CADENCE. The extra quality, expression and animation given to the rhythm and to each successive footfall by increased upward impulsion.

BEND. The lateral curve in the neck and body of the horse.

FLEXION. The articulation, lateral or direct, of the horse's head and/or jaw in relation to its junction with the neck at the poll.

ENGAGEMENT (of quarters). The 'stepping under' of the hind legs which enables the horse to employ the power of his quarters more effectively.

SUSPENSION. The moment during which all four legs of the horse are simultaneously above the ground.

ELEVATION (of the paces). The degree to which a horse raises his feet above the ground during a step or stride (especially in piaffe or passage).

ON THE BIT (to the bit). The condition when the horse, with his head at or near the vertical, the poll unresistant and the mouth soft, takes a steady, equal and relaxed contact with the reins.

TO THE AIDS. A horse is 'to the aids' when he is alert, responsive and obedient to the slightest demands of the rider.

Index

*Note: Italicised figures refer to
illustrations on page cited*